"Every couple needs to soak up every page."

Dr. Tim Clinton, president, American Association of
Christian Counselors; author, *Turn Your Life Around*

"We all want to be well-prepared for a coming baby, but what
about after the baby arrives? Dr. Crawford walks you through
this family transition time with ease and grace, giving practical
and useful help."

Linda S. Mintle, PhD, PureMedia Group, Inc.;
author, *Divorce Proofing Your Marriage*

"When my son and his wife were expecting their first child, I
said to him: 'You have no idea how a baby will change your life.'
How I wish I could have simply handed him this book by my
respected friend and colleague. I know this subject has been on
Mark's heart for a long time, and I am delighted to see his passion
to help couples preserve and nurture their marriage, while joining
the fraternity of parenthood, in print. I can say unreservedly that
it should go on the 'must read' list for every couple expecting a
baby, and it will also be a valuable resource for those who have
already found themselves treading water while trying to survive
the transition from couple to parent."

Freda V. Crews, DMin, PhD, licensed professional counselor;
host, *Time for Hope* TV talk show

"With joy and anticipation, couples go to great lengths to prepare for their new roles and responsibilities as parents. Unfortunately, they're often blindsided by the enormous impact that the birth of a baby inevitably has on their marital relationship. In his book *When Two Become Three*, Dr. Mark Crawford reveals the problems and pitfalls that can threaten even the strongest and most loving relationship. With a compassionate, common-sense approach, Dr. Crawford shows couples how to make the challenging transition from partners to parents and offers them practical ways to nurture the love and intimacy that brought them together in the first place. *When Two Become Three* is an invaluable tool for new parents who want to give their children and their spouses the greatest gift of all: the gift of a happy, healthy marriage."

Rallie McAllister, MD, MPH, MSEH;
author and nationally syndicated columnist for Your Health

"*When Two Become Three* contains rock-solid, practical advice for both new and experienced parents. The greatest gift you can give your kids is a strong, healthy marriage that lasts a lifetime. Mark Crawford shows you how in this wonderful book. If your goal is to maintain a strong, intimate marriage as you raise your family, then consider this book *required reading!*"

Tommy Newberry, author,
The 4:8 Principle and *Success Is Not an Accident*

When Two
Become Three

When Two Become Three

Nurturing Your Marriage
After Baby Arrives

Mark E. Crawford, PhD

Revell
Grand Rapids, Michigan

Published by Fleming H. Revell
a division of Baker Publishing Group
P.O. Box 6287, Grand Rapids, MI 49516-6287
www.revellbooks.com

Printed in the United States of America

Library of Congress Cataloging-in-Publication Data
Crawford, Mark E.
    When two become three : nurturing your marriage after baby arrives / Mark E. Crawford.
        p.   cm.
    Includes bibliographical references.
    ISBN 10: 0-8007-3191-3 (pbk.)
    ISBN 978-0-8007-3191-5 (pbk.)
    1. Marriage. 2. Parenthood. 3. Parents—Psychology. 4. Spouses—Psychology. 5. Parent and infant. I. Title.
HQ734.C885 2007
646.7'8—dc22   2007005483

Several vignettes of couples and excerpts of sessions from the author's practice are used throughout this text to help illustrate points. While the vignettes are real, all names used in these examples are fictitious. Additionally, specific identifying information, such as occupations, has been changed to protect the confidentiality of individuals.

To my parents, Edward and Joan Crawford,
who celebrated fifty years of marriage on October 5, 2006.
Happy Anniversary!
I am proud of you both, and I love you very much.

Contents

Introduction   11

1. The Journey Begins: When Two Become Three . . .   15
2. Communication and Conflict: Working Out the
   Kinks   27
3. Feeling the Pressure: Handling Increased
   Responsibility   61
4. Dividing the Chores: Who Does What Now?   81
5. Some Advice for Moms   99
6. For Dads: Man to Man   115
7. "You've Lost That Loving Feeling": What Happened to
   Sex?   127
8. Friends and Family: How Having a Baby Affects the Rest
   of Your Relationships   143
9. When Worlds Collide: Establishing a Parenting
   Philosophy   159
10. Juggling on a Tightrope: Special Issues with
    Stepfamilies   169

The Journey Continues: Final Thoughts   185
Acknowledgments   187
References   189

Introduction

A strong case can be made that becoming a parent is one of life's most exciting and life-changing experiences. No job is more important, and no task as potentially rewarding and fulfilling as raising a child. Research shows that 90 percent of married couples ultimately have children together. Studies of couples also tell us that anticipating children is an exciting time, and most couples believe that becoming a parent will add a great deal of joy and meaning to their lives. Most parents eagerly anticipate the journey into parenthood and read books and even attend classes to prepare them for their new role. Whether you plan for years to have children or the stork arrives at your doorstep with little warning, expanding your family from a happy couple to a family of three or more is a joyous and exciting transition. And whether your first experience as parents is with one baby, twins, triplets, or even more, the principles contained in this book will be applicable for you. Of course, parents of multiple births face unique challenges in terms of childcare. But in every case there is, however, one major aspect of this transition that new parents do not anticipate and sufficiently prepare for: the impact of children on the marital relationship. Revising an old saying: "First comes love, then comes marriage, then . . . you don't send me flowers anymore!"

Having children is wonderful and can, indeed, add joy and meaning to your life unlike any other experience. However, it is important to understand how your relationship with your spouse is likely to change as well. Several studies indicate that having children can, in fact, be a stressful transition and can actually result in increased conflict for a couple and a decrease in overall marital satisfaction. If you and your spouse prepare for the changes, you can avoid some of the problems that many couples face and continue to grow closer to one another than ever before as you transition into parenthood.

I have written this book to help you with the transition to parenthood. Specifically, this book will help you identify the common challenges to your relationship that typically accompany the metamorphosis from partner to parent. If you desire to keep your relationship strong, loving, and intimate as you raise your children, this book is for you. I am a clinical psychologist with over seventeen years of experience working with families. I am also a husband who is very much in love with my wife and the proud father of two wonderful boys. The content of this book is based on several well-designed scientific studies of couples along with my professional experience as a practicing psychologist and my personal experience as a husband and father. It is my hope that through reading this book you will learn how to protect your marriage from the inevitable challenges of parenting.

———

Confidentiality Note: Several vignettes of couples and excerpts of sessions from my practice are used throughout this text to help illustrate points. While the vignettes are real, all names used in these examples are fictitious. Additionally, specific identifying information, such as occupations, has been changed to protect the confidentiality of individuals.

Style Note: In order to make the text more readable, gender specific pronouns are sometimes used interchangeably. In other words, either *he* is used in one section or *she* is used in another, instead of *he or she* in every case. Except when referring to obvious gender specific topics, the reader should assume that *he* could just as well refer to *she* and vice versa.

1

The Journey Begins

When Two Become Three . . .

When Dana and I were expecting the birth of our first son, we debated the philosophy of childproofing our home. Some of our friends and family espoused the view that children should be taught from day one that the parents are in charge and that children must learn what they can and cannot touch. Others suggested that young children lack the capacity to suppress their natural curiosity and to create an environment that invited constant "No, don't touch" messages would be psychologically harmful. When Caleb arrived, it was clear that he received a generous dose of his father's "high energy / high curiosity" genes. Consequently, the decision of whether to childproof or not was made *for* rather than *by* us (assuming we wanted anything of value to last more than fifteen minutes). We determined that our son was not destructive out of any character defect or malicious intent, but rather by virtue of the fact that he simply was. (I break things, therefore I am.)

As parents, Dana and I quickly learned that it was important to take steps to childproof our home. Obviously, part of this effort was designed to protect our new baby. For example, we put plastic plugs into all the outlets, moved out of reach anything small enough to put in a crawler's mouth, and put locks on cabinets with cleaning supplies or other toxic substances. We never knew there were so many hazards awaiting a newborn in our own home. Spend a few minutes in the section of the store that sells safety equipment for toddlers and you'll start feeling that your home is about as safe for your child as a nuclear waste site.

In addition, we took steps to protect anything "fragile" that a baby might destroy out of curiosity. Gone were any breakable table decorations, plant stands that would topple as a toddler might try to pull up to take a few steps, and cute little ticking clocks that begged to be disassembled. The effort we expended to keep the valuable things (I'm talking phones and clocks, not antiques and heirlooms) out of his path of unintentional destruction paid off by not having to constantly repair and replace items.

Just as a new child in a home represents a threat to the house (not out of any malicious motive but just because he is there), so the arrival of a newborn presents an intense and often unrecognized "threat" to a marriage. I know many of you (especially you parents-to-be) are thinking, *Shame on you! Children are a gift from God and should be cherished.* I couldn't agree with you more. Children are one of God's greatest gifts to any couple and should certainly be cherished and appreciated. At the same time, becoming a parent will rock your world so much that it is naïve to think that it won't affect your relationship with your spouse. The bad news is that if you fail to consider and prepare for just how much having children can affect your marital relationship, the "happily-ever-after" ending you hope for may be more difficult to find than you think. Consider the following data:

- A ten-year longitudinal study of couples showed that 92 percent of new parents described more conflict and disagreement after they had a baby than prior to becoming parents (Cowan & Cowan, 2000).
- The same longitudinal study of well-functioning couples having a first baby showed that 12.5 percent had separated or divorced by the time their first baby was one-and-a-half years old. If the divorce rate is around 50 percent nationally, then it appears that roughly one-fourth of all divorces take place before their first child is one-and-a-half years old (Cowan & Cowan, 2000).
- Marital conflict increases by a factor of nine after the birth of the first child (Belsky & Kelly, 1994).
- After the birth of a first baby, marital conflict and disagreement increased in nine out of ten couples studied (Cowan, 1997).
- Several studies indicate that after the first child is born, couples report and demonstrate fewer positive and/or affectionate interactions with each other (Cox, Paley, Payne, & Burchinal, 1999; Kurdek, 1993; MacDermid, Huston, & McHale, 1990).
- One group of researchers found that as the demands of parenting increase, many couples report less intimacy and less of a sense of "togetherness" and that these changes actually begin to cause them to redefine their marriage (Belsky, Spanier, & Rovine, 1983; Belsky, Lang, & Rovine, 1985).

- Conversation and sexual activity decline dramatically after the first child is born (Belsky & Kelly, 1994).

- 40 percent of all children born into two-parent homes will live in a single-parent home by the time they are eighteen years old (Glick & Lin, 1986).

In over seventeen years of working with families, I have seen far too many parents fail to nurture their marital relationship following the birth of their first child. In the words of one of my colleagues, Dr. John Lochridge, "New parents spend all of their time parenting and not enough time 'spousing.'" For many couples, becoming new parents ultimately begins a gradual neglect of the basic essential ingredients of sustaining a vital, healthy, and intimate marriage, resulting in significant marital discord, divorce, or the realization after the children have left home many years later that they are married to someone they barely know. In my experience, many couples transitioning to the "empty nest" phase of life are stunned to realize how little they have invested in their marital relationship during their parenting phase of life, and the void that exists after their last child leaves home for college is painfully evident.

Smart people plan for years to provide financial security in their golden years. They meet annually with financial advisors to make sure that they are "on track" to meet their financial goals. They make regular monthly deposits into retirement accounts in order to meet the goal of financial security when they are older. However, these same smart individuals don't even think about their future relationship goals with their spouse. Furthermore, they make few, if any, deposits into their marital relationship "account" and are surprised when there are few positive feelings left when they reach the empty nest phase of life. In fact, some couples are financially well-off but relationally bankrupt in their later years. This tragic scenario is avoidable with a little awareness and planning.

Recently, I was being interviewed on a radio program on the topic of maintaining a high quality marriage and presented the above analogy. A caller objected to viewing his marriage like a business arrangement and felt that my model did not allow him and his wife to view their marriage as a journey to be taken together. While I understand his point, I would add that it is also important to plan for journeys. A relational journey is a process that can be spontaneous and fun. At the same time, failure to intentionally invest in the health of the relationship by purposefully making regular deposits of time, affection, attention, and the other things necessary for an intimate relationship to grow and thrive will decrease the quality of the journey and may increase the risk of not even finishing the journey together.

For the sake of clarity, I feel the need to reiterate the fact that I love children, and I *love* being a father. The blessing of being a dad has brought me tremendous joy. I cannot imagine my life without my boys, and I thank God every day for the privilege of being a father to Caleb and Ben. It is *because* I love them so very much that I believe it is vital that their mother and I have a great marriage to each other. I believe that if they grow up in a home where their parents really love and enjoy each other, they will be happier and healthier boys and will grow up to be happier and healthier men. I also believe that if they grow up in a home where their mom and dad really love each other and enjoy an intimate and healthy relationship, they will be better equipped to establish and maintain a marriage for themselves that will be fulfilling and will last a lifetime. When they reach the age when they consider marriage, it is my hope that they will look back and think, *I hope when I get married, my wife and I are as happy together as Mom and Dad!*

It is important to understand that investing the proper amount of time parenting while simultaneously investing in and nurturing a great marriage can be a challenge. The good news from all the studies on couples becoming parents is that those couples who have made an effort to attend to and work on their relationship are much more likely to make the transition to parenthood without a serious negative impact upon their marriage. In fact, some couples actually reported that having children enhanced their relationship and that they grew closer to one another as they became parents. It is my hope that this book will help couples realize that while planning and starting a family is indeed one of the peak experiences of life, it also requires that new parents understand the toll that the transition to parenthood exacts on a marriage. It requires effort to make sure that the marital relationship stays strong and healthy.

The very things you took for granted in the prechild years of your marriage (e.g., time to talk, shared experiences, a healthy sex life, well-defined roles, etc.) get taken for granted or turned upside down as you transition into parenthood. New parents are inundated with myriad advice from everyone they know (and many people they don't know) on every topic from discipline to breastfeeding to sleep patterns of newborns. However, I submit that one piece of advice to new parents that is worth considering is to make sure you attend to your marriage. Keep your marital relationship strong, intimate, and nourished. The book *What to Expect When You're Expecting* seems to be a fixture on the New York Times Bestseller List—and for good reason. It's a very helpful book, and every new parent wants to be as prepared as possible for the arrival of their new baby. Properly preparing for your newborn also requires you to anticipate the challenges to your marital relationship and develop some tools for coping with the changes that lie ahead.

There are many reasons I believe that this is an often overlooked but extremely important issue. The research on couples clearly shows that there is a strong relationship between unhappiness in a marriage and separation and divorce (as if you needed scientific studies to tell you that!). What you may not have known is that research also shows that people who are unhappy in their marriages also suffer worse emotional and even physical health. Unhappy marriages also are more likely to contribute to less effective parenting and may even negatively affect child development in certain areas.

What about the effects of divorce on children? I assume that if you are reading this book, you want to stay married to your spouse. Divorce is painful for everyone involved. The research regarding the effects of divorce on children is not especially encouraging. While there appears to be no *universal* set of problems associated with children of divorce, studies suggest that children of divorce may be at greater risk of experiencing depression, academic under-achievement, feelings of guilt over having caused the divorce, fears of abandonment, immaturity, anger, and other problems. It should be noted that not all children from divorced families exhibit problems like these. There are many factors which contribute to the negative effects of divorce on children, including ongoing conflict between divorced parents following the divorce, the loss of time with one or both parents (usually the father), and less effective parenting secondary to the painful effects of the divorce on the parents themselves. The most important thing parents can do following a divorce to buffer their children from the negative effects is to bury the hatchet and work together cooperatively to co-parent their children.

For couples who do avoid divorce, research also supports the benefits of raising children within the context of a happy home. One study of preschool-aged children showed that preschoolers raised in homes with a lot of marital conflict had higher levels of stress hormones compared with other children. Furthermore, by the time these same children who grew up with battling parents were fifteen years of age, they showed more truancy, depression, peer rejection, behavioral problems, low achievement, and school failure than a comparable group of teenagers. Therefore, just "sticking it out" and avoiding divorce does not guarantee a great environment in which to raise your kids. Raising children in the context of a happy marriage is the equivalent of raising plants in a greenhouse—the optimal environment within which to grow and develop.

Most couples obviously want a satisfying marriage during and long after the child-rearing years. Recent research by John Gottman, PhD, has revealed that a pervasive attribute of marriages in which both couples express a great deal of contentment is that the relationship is based on a deep friendship, which he defines as a mutual respect and enjoyment of each other's company. While this may sound self-evident, the simple fact that escapes most couples is that this type of relationship requires *effort and attention*. Relationships are living and dynamic entities that require ongoing attention. Neglect them and, like a plant that receives no water, they will shrivel up and eventually die. Unfortunately, it is too easy to begin to neglect each other following the birth of a child. The type of friendship based on mutual respect and enjoyment of each other's company that seems to be the sine qua non of a happy marriage will not continue without making the marriage a priority at a time when resources are limited and energy is low.

Another reason to nurture the marital relationship during the child-raising years is to provide a good role model for the children.

In my work with young adults who are unmarried and struggling to find a fulfilling, intimate relationship, I often hear them say, "I think it would be easier if I knew what a healthy relationship was supposed to be like. I sure don't want to end up in a marriage like my parents had." Often this is said with a great deal of sadness rather than anger. Many young adults look back at their parents' marriage and see two people living parallel lives, sharing responsibilities and a commitment, but in a relationship without any real intimacy or joy. While these young adults appreciate and value their parents' commitment to each other and to the children, they simply want more for themselves. In other words, they want a marriage that will last a lifetime but one that will also be fun! I think a helpful question to consider in the early years of parenting is "What kind of example of a marital relationship will I want my children to think of when they are in their twenties?" Think for a moment of the adjectives you would like for your child to use if someone were to ask her to tell about your marriage to your spouse. Whatever terms you came up with, let me assure you that your marriage will not magically turn out this way. You will have to make a conscious decision to work at the relationship *starting now* and to continue to make this a priority during the next several years.

Finally, it is important to attend to your marriage in the early years of parenting because you are investing now for the time when your children leave home. I have never met an individual who planned to marry, have children, then divorce. Everyone I know plans for their marriage to last a lifetime. When you consider the time span this includes, you really spend only a fraction of your marriage in the parenting years. Oh sure, you will always be a parent even when your children are in their thirties, but certainly not in the same way. In fact, once your child enters adolescence, your role as parent begins to shift from a direct, decision-making mode to a more overseeing, consulting type of mode. Children must learn the skills of self-governing behavior and independent decision making before they can leave home as autonomous adults. This means a gradual handing over of responsibilities during adolescence. Thus, the role of parenting is a rapidly evolving one. While the early years of parenting can feel overwhelming and all-consuming on the best days, you actually spend only a relatively brief period of your entire marriage in this role. As I mentioned earlier, I have counseled many couples in the "empty nest" stage of life who feel disconnected from one another and admit that when the children first arrived, they allowed parenting and career building to consume most of their energy. This resulted in a neglect of their marital relationship that began a process of erosion of the intimacy that existed before they had children.

Joe and Tina are typical of many couples I see in my office. Joe is a successful financial planner, and Tina spent that last twenty-three years raising their two children and maintaining their home. They came in to see me because neither of them is really happy in their marriage. Their youngest daughter left for college eighteen months ago, and since then they feel that most of the time they are living parallel lives. There is not much fighting or arguing, but there is not much intimacy either.

Joe comes home from work and gets on the computer while Tina watches her favorite TV show or reads. Joe gets up early to exercise before work, so he usually is in bed by 9:30 or 10:00 p.m., and Tina doesn't feel ready to turn in until after 11:00 p.m. Joe leaves in the morning before Tina gets up. Tina's day is busy, but since she doesn't work, Joe laments, "What in the world is she doing all day long?" Because they don't really interact much in the evening, they share few details with each other about how their day was spent. Weekends may find them going out to dinner with another couple; but Joe talks with the guy and Tina interacts mostly with the other woman. Joe plays golf all day Sunday and Tina has other interests. It's no wonder they are feeling disconnected. They are doing well financially, so they don't fight about money. The children are off to college, so they don't really argue about parenting issues. In fact, they don't argue much at all—there's just this . . . space between them. They are both starting to wonder, "What's the point of staying together?" Joe has confided to me privately that he is starting to have stronger thoughts that if he met the right person, he'd be a lot happier. He quickly compliments Tina on what a great mother she has been over the years, but in retrospect, he thinks that for the last several years, the kids are all they had in common. Now that they're gone, he wonders why he should stay in the marriage at all. Tina feels sad that Joe is so unhappy. However, she too acknowledges that she hasn't felt close to Joe in years. In fact, she's surprised that her reaction to Joe's questioning the marriage isn't causing her to be more upset.

Joe and Tina exemplify the kind of marital neglect that is common among couples. If they get a divorce, it will shock even their closest friends. On the surface, everything looks fine, but deep down, there is a real problem. This type of marital crisis is very similar to the health threats posed by chronic high blood pressure. There are few symptoms, and the person can look very healthy. However, one day, the results can show up in the form of a fatal crisis. In my field, we talk about the "health" of a marriage. Just as an individual must live a healthy lifestyle on a daily basis in order to maintain physical health, a couple must live a healthy lifestyle *as a couple* in order to maintain a healthy relationship.

Most people are in the best position to enjoy the fruits of their labor after their children leave home. They are often financially better off than when they started their marriage, and they have more free time as the demands of the early years of parenting and career building have lessened. If a couple has fed and nourished a healthy and intimate marital relationship during the parenting years, they can now enjoy this next stage together with their partner—a partner with whom they have shared many challenges, weathered many storms, and shared incomparable joys. As a bonus, I have found that young adults who are preparing to leave home generally feel much better about leaving if they believe their parents will be fulfilled and happy after they leave. I have had many young adults share with me that they actually worry about leaving home because they wonder what their parents will do after they don't have anyone to look after. One of these young adults summed it up well when he said, "If my parents had a life, I'd feel a lot better about going out and getting one of my own."

Just as Dana and I conducted a thorough survey of our home when we became parents to identify the areas most vulnerable to a young child's natural intense curiosity, I want to help you take a close look at your marital relationship in order to identify the areas that may be "vulnerable" to having young children in your home—vulnerable in the sense that the finite resources available to a couple (e.g., time, physical energy, and emotional energy) must be reallocated and managed differently to make sure that the marriage does not suffer neglect. The chapters that follow identify some key areas that research, as well as my clinical and personal experience, suggests are issues that should be discussed. I will identify how the introduction of a young child into a family may "stress" the marital relationship in several areas. I will also offer some advice on how to protect your marriage from these stresses so you and your spouse can enjoy a healthy, intimate, and strong relationship.

Remember, a good marriage is one gift that benefits everyone in your family.

2

Communication and Conflict

Working Out the Kinks

Communication. If there's one thing couples believe they need to work on (whether they are parents or not) it is learning how to communicate better. Older theories of marriage held that the root of all evil in troubled marriages was poor communication and poor conflict resolution skills. This theory influenced the practice of marriage therapists for decades as skilled therapists attempted to teach Bob and Katy how to really listen to each other and to communicate more clearly. Early in my career, I spent many hours with couples teaching them techniques such as reflective listening (e.g., "What I hear you saying is . . .") and making "I statements" (e.g., getting them to change "*You* make me feel . . ." to "When you do that *I* feel . . ."). More recent and refined research by people like John Gottman, PhD suggest that while communication is important, it is not the fountainhead of marital bliss we once believed it to be. Thus, while Bob and Katy could now carry on a pretty good give-and-take conversation using "I statements" and hearing what one another said, there were still some patterns that needed to be recognized and changed before conflict was less of a threat to their relationship.

All couples bump into problems in the areas of communication and resolving conflict with one another, and there are definitely better and worse ways of doing both. Whether or not you feel you had problems as a couple in this area before becoming parents, research suggests that you can expect conflict to increase shortly after you become parents. One study indicated that 92 percent of couples said they had more disagreement and conflict in their marriage after becoming parents than they did before (Cowan & Cowan, 2000).

This makes sense when you think about it. First, there's more to disagree about. From choosing a middle name to deciding how long (if at all) to let the baby cry before rushing into the nursery on a rescue mission, there are myriad decisions on which you and your spouse will try to reach consensus as new parents. Good luck agreeing on all of them without some healthy conflict. Second, having a child of your own intensifies things. You may have been able to give in or let certain issues slide that were not a big deal before. However, once you become a parent, these ostensibly small decisions feel enormous. New parents can get a little crazy about things like how important breast milk versus formula is to the child's overall development and future. You used to laugh at how neurotic other parents would get about little things like whether or not their child was eating enough, but your day is coming. Disagreements about your child can take on the feel of a Supreme Court decision that will determine the course of history for generations to come.

Third, you are probably just plain worn out in the first few months of parenthood. Getting up in the middle of the night, not being able to sleep in on the weekend, and the new routines all lead to fatigue. We all know how cranky and impatient we can get when we are tired. Finally, we know from research that couples report a decline in shared leisure time, general companionship, and intimacy in the early months of parenting. There is simply less opportunity for small talk and conversing with each other. This results in a decreased feeling of connectedness and fewer overall positive feelings about each other in general. The benefit of the doubt is a bit harder to find in disagreements. Furthermore, it may begin to feel like "all we do is fight" since there may be fewer neutral or positive interchanges with each other relative to conflicts and arguments. Before you were parents, a fun day at the park or a night of hot sex could really make up for the last bad fight. When the fun days and hot nights move from short-term to long-term memory, the conflict seems more painful and long-lasting. These are but a few of the many things that contribute to more disagreements and conflict in the early months of parenting.

Dan and Linda

Dan and Linda were typical of many new parents I see in my practice. Dan was a highly successful developer who worked long hours in an intense environment. He took big but calculated risks to close deals that netted him a nice take-home paycheck. However, as with most of these types of jobs, his neck was on the line constantly and he felt the pressure. Linda was a relatively new stay-at-home mom. She enjoyed taking care of their son, and she had her own routine at home. Dan's income provided more than enough to allow

Linda to stay home with Josh. Furthermore, Dan liked the fact that Josh was being raised by his mother rather than paid-for child-care. For the most part, they had reached an agreement regarding who did what inside and outside of the house. Dan worked hard and provided very comfortably while Linda took care of Josh and made sure that Dan came home to a meal at the end of the day. They were even able to pay for cleaners to do most of the housecleaning.

Dan and Linda's conflict had to do with household chores, but the problem was less with "who does what" than with "thoughtfulness." There were a few tasks around the house that Linda simply couldn't do by herself. These involved some heavy lifting and other things she needed Dan to do. Dan did not object to doing these things. However, his sense of urgency about them was very different from Linda's. One day in my office, the tension boiled over.

Linda: Dan, you just don't care about me at all.

Dan: Linda, what are you talking about? [*looking and sounding defeated and exasperated*]

Linda: You know that I can't hang that picture by myself and it's been sitting there for three weeks.

Dan: Well why didn't you remind me to hang it?

Linda: Why should I have to remind you? You know I need to have it hung—I've told you several times. If you cared about anyone other than yourself, you'd just hang it.

Dan: [*Looking at me*] This is what ticks me off. Do you know how many things I have on my desk when I walk into my office that if I don't get done could cost me a contract? [*After seeing me redirect him to Linda, Dan looks at Linda*] Do you?

Linda: Do you know how many things *I* have to do all day long. While you're at work having business lunches and meetings, *I'm* here taking care of *your* son. Do *I* get any credit for that?

Dan: Look, I appreciate what you do for Josh and for me, but you just . . .

Linda: [*Interrupting Dan*] No you don't—if you did, you'd take care of the few things I ask you to do.

Dan: [*Raising his voice*] I told you I would hang the stupid picture—I just need you to remind me. I don't see what's so unreasonable about that. I have a lot on my mind.

Linda: And it's not me. Just forget it!

I have hundreds of examples I could have used from my practice, but this one is typical of the way couples often engage in conflict and disagreement. There are many layers of issues for both of them that could be explored and discussed within this seemingly simple argument. For example, Linda is feeling less important since she has taken on a new role of stay-at-home mom. She has less contact with her friends, less time to work out, she rarely puts on makeup or dresses up (what's the point?), and Dan has admittedly spent more time at work. Linda is an attractive and intelligent woman. Before becoming a full-time mom, she used to dress sharply, and she got a lot of attention and admiring glances from others. She also interacted more with adults, and this reinforced the fact that she usually had something valuable to contribute to conversations. The things that used to make her feel good about herself are suddenly in short supply. Her self-esteem has dropped a few notches. A few months ago, an unhung picture would not have been as big a deal to her. She would have been less sensitive to Dan's lack of responsiveness to her request, and probably would have just continued to remind him until he hung the picture—which he would have done eventually.

On the other hand, Dan is feeling greater pressure than ever. He has always been driven to earn and save money. He has provided a nice lifestyle for Linda and himself, and he always felt proud of what he was able to do for them. Since Linda has been preoccupied with Josh, he has felt unappreciated for his efforts. To make things worse, he has started thinking about braces, college tuition, and how much more vacations will cost with an additional family member. To compound the stress, the deals he works on now are bigger than ever, and there's more "skin in the game" for him. He feels the need to work more and earn more. Privately, he admits that he should have hung the picture, but he feels overwhelmed and hates being "nagged all the time."

These are the issues that need to be discussed but rarely are in the typical couple's argument. Too often, people wait until their feelings boil over and come on full force with accusations and assumptions. This is called "store and dump": i.e., one person stores up anger, frustration, and everything else until they can no longer hold it in, and then they find the most inopportune time to dump all of this onto their spouse. The response is generally defensiveness rather than being heard and understood, and a fight ensues that leaves both feeling angry and hurt. Pretty soon, one or both will begin to pull away to avoid the pain of the unresolved conflict.

It's Not What You Say but How You Say It

Lots of people feel that the key to getting along better with each other is to come to an agreement or compromise when problems arise. While it doesn't hurt to reach agreement and resolve differences with each other, it's less important than you think. In fact, research on new parents indicated that whether or not a problem was resolved during discussions was far less important to how they felt about their overall relationship than *how they felt about the process of talking about the problem* (Ball, 1984). Moms are probably nodding right now while dads are scratching their heads. It seems that if Jack and Dianne have a disagreement but can walk away feeling good about how the discussion went *whether or not they resolved it,* they both will feel better about their relationship, and the marriage is stronger.

Clearly, some types of disagreements in a marriage require a specific solution or behavioral change. For example, if one person consistently spends beyond an agreed upon budget and places the family at financial risk, simply talking about the problem will not be sufficient. However, most things about which couples fight and on which they get "stuck" are what author Dan Wile refers to as perpetual problems that really don't have or require an easily identified specific solution. In those cases, it is important that couples develop a way to discuss these issues in a way that allows them to make room for individual differences in their relationship and to feel okay about how things are talked about. Let's talk about how to make sure that happens.

Anatomy of an Argument: What Goes Wrong?

Couples everywhere owe their gratitude to Dr. John Gottman for his excellent research on couples. He has identified several key areas that couples should be aware of when it comes to communication and conflict. I strongly recommend that couples read his book *The Seven Principles for Making Marriage Work* for a complete understanding of his work and how it can be applied to their relationship. I will borrow heavily on his work to offer some pointers on communication and conflict here.

First, let's talk about what to avoid. Dr. Gottman identified four behaviors that are certain to lead couples down the wrong road. He refers to them as the Four Horsemen of the Apocalypse (Four Horsemen for short). They are (1) criticism, (2) defensiveness, (3) stonewalling, and (4) contempt. Briefly, here's what each refers to:

1. *Criticism* is a global and personal attack on a person's character or personality. It differs from a simple complaint which references a behavior. For example, a complaint (which is okay) would be, "I am annoyed because you left the wet towel on the bed again," while a criticism would be, "You are a thoughtless and selfish person, expecting me to pick up your wet towel."

2. *Defensiveness* is usually a response to criticism. It refers to a person responding to a criticism or even a complaint by defending himself or herself rather than validating the issue and accepting the feedback.

3. *Stonewalling* is when one person just "checks out" of the conversation. He or she stops fighting or even talking and shuts down completely. In extreme forms, the person just walks out altogether.

4. *Contempt* is a behavior or comment that conveys disgust or disdain toward the other person. It includes such things as sarcasm, cynicism, mocking, name-calling, and so forth. Contempt is the worst of the Four Horsemen in terms of outcome in a marriage. Couples who behave contemptuously toward each other appear to be traveling in the HOV lane toward divorce unless they change this pattern of interaction.

34

Almost every couple engages in some of these behaviors from time to time. I have had numerous couples come to me after I have recommended Dr. Gottman's book and lament, "Is there any hope for us? We do all of those Horse thingies!" The problem is not whether a couple is occasionally critical, defensive, or even contemptuous. The real trouble comes when couples *regularly* interact with these patterns. Don't feel doomed if one or more of these Horsemen occasionally gallops through your relationship. The goal is to make them as infrequent as possible (i.e., don't let them graze in your pasture). In order to illustrate how couples engage in patterns involving these toxic styles of relating to one another, let's have a look at them in action.

Mike and Deborah

Mike is a corporate attorney for a large firm. He is a typical type-A guy, and it has paid off in his career. He is successful by most standards, but he never feels satisfied that he is. Deborah is a former CPA with plenty of experience and a successful track record of her own. She took some time off after giving birth to Jennifer, their daughter, but is now working part-time. Her career allows for flexibility, and the return to part-time work is exactly what Mike and Deborah planned for. Jennifer spends two days a week with Deborah's mother, and a nanny comes to the house for another half day when Deborah works from home, catching up on emails and paperwork. They would say that they've made the transition to parenthood fine, but there are some issues that have created some conflict. The argument they've been having lately is about money. Mike thinks that Deborah spends far too much money on clothes for Jennifer that she will wear only a few times before they no longer fit. Deborah cannot see why

Mike is worried about how much she spends on clothing their daughter when he doesn't hesitate to shell out plenty of money on his hobby—fishing.

Deborah: You're the most self-centered jerk I've ever met. You don't have a problem spending thousands of dollars on sport fishing trips, but you want me to dress our daughter like a war orphan. [*This comment actually is a two-for-one bonus: there's contempt and criticism rolled into one. Calling Mike a "self-centered jerk" is clearly contempt and her comment about his hobby is more of a personal criticism than a complaint.*]

Mike: Being out of the business world has made you stupid. You have to know that fishing is one way I meet and entertain clients. How do you expect me to pay the bills around here if I don't keep growing my business? [*Mike is fighting contempt with contempt by calling Deborah "stupid." He's also responding with defensiveness rather than trying to understand what Deborah is so upset about. In other words, he's defending his actions rather than trying to understand Deborah's point of view.*]

Deborah: [*Recognizing that this is escalating and needs to be discussed more rationally*] Look Mike, I really don't care how much you spend on fishing. Just don't tell me that I'm spending too much on Jennifer. We can afford it, so what's the big deal?

Mike: [*Missing his opportunity to discuss things more calmly*] The big deal is that I want to retire someday, and the way you're burning through money means I'll be working until Jennifer draws social security. Besides, you just think you have to dress her in baby Neiman clothes to impress your friends. I don't care what they think. [*Mike has remained in his defensive posture and makes no effort to de-escalate the emotion and conflict.*]

Deborah: Well you sure seem to care what *your* friends think. How much did you spend last weekend when you took them all out to lunch? And by the way, how many beers did you guys drink while you were there? [*This is a frequently seen phenomenon of including yet another issue into an already heated discussion. Not only is Deborah upset that Mike is criticizing her spending habits as well as spending time away on a hobby she really sees as selfish and unnecessary, she now takes the opportunity to let him know that she disapproves of the fact that she thinks Mike drinks too much when he's with his friends.*] You guys are like a bunch of fraternity brothers who still think they're in college. When are you going to grow up? [*More criticism*]

Mike: [*Looking at me*] I'm not having this discussion. [*After this he looks at his watch and walks out—stonewalling. Mike is clearly overwhelmed at this point by Deborah's high level of emotion, and the number of issues she is bringing up. He also feels attacked because she is bringing up issues (all of which have some validity) in a critical manner. Mike is flooded.*]

Deborah: [*Dissolves into tears*] He's such a jerk. [*Now Deborah feels invalidated and abandoned. Mike's walking out of the session is not seen as his effort to avoid feeling overwhelmed but as a sign that he doesn't care about how she feels or even about the relationship.*]

37

Under the Surface—What Else Is Going On?

Watching a couple who are arguing like Mike and Deborah is a bit like watching a head-on collision in slow motion. But there are some things going on under the surface that need to be understood before the destructive pattern can be changed. Research tells us that women tend to bring up problems more often and talk more in the first few minutes of a conversation than men. We also know that, in general, men talk in order to solve problems and exchange meaningful or relevant information whereas women talk in order to establish or to extend intimacy. When couples are studied while discussing disagreements, we also find that men try to maintain a one-up position and rarely reveal their vulnerabilities while women try to increase "evenness" in conversations and reveal their vulnerabilities more in order to preserve the relationship. Men tend to value autonomy more and women tend to value connectedness more. To put this in everyday terms: (a) women talk in order to relate and men talk in order to problem-solve, and (b) men worry about "losing" an argument more than women and will react more defensively when they feel like they are being attacked or are about to lose.

We also know that when faced with conflict, men and women react much differently inside. For example, when conflict arises, men tend to become emotionally flooded more easily than women. In other words, they experience a "fight or flight" response quickly when they experience conflict. This refers to a biological reaction during which the brain sends out certain neurotransmitters that increase a man's heart rate and blood pressure. They are preparing to fight off an attack or run for their lives. As a result, during conflicts in relationships, men tend to become more rational and avoidant in order to protect against feeling flooded. To a woman, this can look like a man is becoming more argumentative (when he resorts to logical and rational debate) or that he doesn't care (when he avoids the discussion). Research tells us that a man's cardiovascular system is more reactive than a female's and is slower to recover from stress. One experiment (Zillman, 1994) showed that when a man was treated rudely by someone and then asked to relax for twenty minutes, his blood pressure surged and stayed elevated until he got a chance to retaliate. Only then was he able to calm down. By contrast, when a woman was treated rudely and then asked to calm down for twenty minutes, she was able to do it. Interestingly, if she was pressured into retaliating, her blood pressure went back up. Men are simply more overwhelmed by conflict in their relationships than women. Thus, they tend to avoid it. All of these facts lead to some interesting dynamics.

When a woman brings up an issue about which she and her husband disagree (which is more common than a man bringing it up according to the research), a man can easily become "flooded" by it. He will instinctively try to problem-solve and "fix" whatever the problem is. This makes sense, because he's trying to make the conflict go away by resolving it. Unfortunately, the woman needs to be heard and may feel interrupted by his rapidly offered solution. Furthermore, a solution offered too quickly often makes her feel that he is minimizing the importance of the issue she is raising to him. When a woman feels that she is not being heard or worse, that she is being invalidated or that her issue is being minimized, she may engage more or turn up the intensity. To the observer, this may look like the woman is becoming more "emotional" in her tone of voice or nonverbal behavior. She may talk more rapidly, more loudly, or in a tone that says, "I'm ticked off." This will very often result in the man moving closer to his "fight or flight" response and closer to a state of emotional "flooding."

At this point, men typically shut down to avoid being flooded or fight back in a defensive manner. Ultimately, the woman feels abandoned or attacked in response to his reaction. Both people walk away feeling worse and the problem remains unaddressed.

Before long, one or both of the couple stops bringing up issues that are likely to result in this painful pattern. This will accomplish the goal of decreasing conflict in the relationship, but at a price. When the couple starts avoiding conflict, they begin to feel disconnected, which results in a decrease in intimacy and overall satisfaction with the relationship. This is the genesis of the worst of all emotions in a marriage—apathy. When I work with couples, the emotion I am most concerned about is not anger, hurt, disappointment, or even betrayal. It is apathy (i.e., they just don't care anymore). Any other emotions suggest that the individuals still care about each other. However, when one or both of the people in a marriage becomes apathetic about the outcome of the relationship, it is a very troubling sign. It is often difficult to reengage a person who is apathetic.

Suggestions for Dealing with Conflict More Effectively

With a few tools and a willingness to approach conflict differently, couples can avoid the patterns described above and feel better about how they talk about the inevitable conflicts that all couples experience. Author Dan Wile accurately points out that all couples have conflicts, miscommunications, and misunderstandings. In fact, he states that when two people get married, they are choosing a set of perpetual problems that will be there for decades—perhaps forever. Many people mistakenly believe that problems in a relationship are a sign that they married the wrong person. This is a naïve and immature view of relationships. Wile says that if you had married someone else, you might not have the *same* problems that you have with your spouse, but you would undoubtedly have *some* set of problems with that person which seem to have no ostensible solution. The key is to accept that you and your spouse will have some things to work out, and the *way* you work them out is much more important than the solutions you come up with for the problems (assuming there are solutions to be found at all).

I tell the couples I work with that there are a few commonly believed "myths of marriage" to avoid. One of them is the belief that "If I had married my 'soulmate,' I wouldn't be having these problems, and I'd really be happy." I believe that a "soulmate" is a misleading and confusing term. Hollywood notions of romance and relationships would have you believe that there's a person out there (or maybe more than one) who is your perfect match. All you have to do is find him or her and relational bliss is just an "I do" away. If you are having problems in your relationship or if you are unhappy, it just means that you didn't marry your soulmate and you need to keep looking. This is simply nonsense. If you want to believe in this concept of a soulmate, let me encourage you to understand that a soulmate is *created* rather than *discovered*. In other words, if you and your spouse make a commitment to spend years together building a family, creating a mission statement, changing and evolving as people, celebrating life's best moments and suffering through life's worst moments *together*, then after many years, you may find that the person you've traveled that journey with is, in fact, your soulmate. You won't, however, *find* your "soulmate" at the other end of a restaurant on a lonely evening and instantly recognize him or her. I mean . . . really. This notion reminds me of a quote from novelist Tom Robbins: "We waste time looking for the perfect lover instead of creating the perfect love."

Once you accept the healthier, more realistic notion that no two people can get married and live together without working out some problems together and that problems in a relationship do *not* mean you've married the wrong person, here are some pointers for dealing with conflict differently:

1. Accept that you and your spouse will disagree on things and will see the world differently.

Again, this is not a sign that you married the wrong person. It is just the way marriages work. If you had married someone just like yourself, you'd be pretty bored. If you constantly see the presence of problems as signs of a malignant tumor in the relationship, you will mistakenly believe that your relationship is terminal and will begin to harbor "toxic thoughts" about your marriage (i.e., thoughts that lead to negative feelings about your spouse and your relationship). Couples who view problems in a relationship as normal are not easily derailed. They see working out problems as just part of the deal—as much a necessary part of life as doing laundry and taking out the trash. No one enjoys these tasks, but everyone accepts them as part of life. In fact, the absence of conflict in a marriage is often a bad sign. When a spouse sees no hope of resolving disagreements, he sometimes gives up or "checks out" and assumes that there's just no point of bringing up any issue since "nothing ever changes." This can lead to apathy, which is the most dangerous of all emotions in any relationship. Another reason some couples have no conflict is that one spouse is afraid to bring up any areas of disagreement for discussion. The person may fear her partner's anger, or she may be so conflict avoidant she would rather suffer in silence than experience conflict with her spouse. This is a recipe for resentment and anger. Constantly acquiescing or making concessions in order to avoid conflict will, over time, lead to some real problems in the relationship.

Karen was a woman who was raised in a home in which her parents fought openly and often. She was traumatized by the overt hostility and combative arguments that her parents displayed in front of her. She vowed that when she became a mother, she would never put her children through the same turmoil. Consequently, she swung to the other end of the continuum. In other words, she avoided all conflict. In order to eliminate conflict from her marriage, she never raised objections to anything her husband Larry did or did not do, even things that she should have called him on. It was a great deal for Larry—sort of.

Larry could pretty much do whatever he wanted. If he wanted to play golf all weekend, Karen raised no objections. He got up from the dinner table each evening and sat in front of the television while Karen (who had prepared dinner) dutifully cleaned up the kitchen and then took care of getting the kids ready for bed. For a while, Larry thought they had the best marriage on the block. Then Karen became less interested in sex. To avoid conflict, she complied with his sexual advances, but Larry knew her heart was not in it. Each day she grew more and more distant. Finally, she confided in a session that she had so many layers of resentment covering her love for Larry that she was wondering if she loved him at all. Larry seemed dumbfounded and asked, "Karen, why didn't you say anything?" She responded, "I knew if I started telling you what was bothering me it would turn into a fight. I'd rather be miserable than have our kids see us fighting with each other." Unfortunately, Karen erroneously believed that all conflict had to be harsh, destructive, and painful. Once we talked about how conflict is necessary to resolve differences and that conflict did not have to be synonymous with domestic warfare, the layers of resentment could be addressed.

2. Realize that some problems just don't have solutions or compromises that are easy to find.

I worked with a couple who disagreed vehemently regarding whether their child should be a vegetarian or not. The difference didn't matter much when they did not have a child. Russell found it intriguing and a bit exotic that Kate was a vegetarian. It was one of her "quirks" that made her that much more attractive to him. Kate, on the other hand, had no problems with Russell's fondness for filet. After all, years ago she'd given up the idea that she'd meet an attractive and successful man who had a sense of humor and was *also* a vegetarian. Her friends and family told her that she didn't need to be so picky and that she'd never get married if she waited for everything to be perfect. Besides, Russell didn't give *her* a hard time about her diet, so why should she tell him how he needed to eat.

All of this changed when Chloe was born. Each was adamant about which of their views was the "right" one and that their daughter should be raised according to the right philosophy. Neither felt that a compromise was possible (you either are or are not vegetarian, according to one or the other of their views), and neither was successful in convincing the other of the "rightness" of his or her respective view. Therefore, they simply had to agree on one way to raise their daughter until she was old enough to make her own decision about this. Because they were able to discuss their feelings without bringing the Four Horsemen into the conversation too often, both were able to feel relatively good about the discussion, despite the lack of consensus in their views. Because it was a bigger deal to one of them, the other was able to recognize this and to concede. They agreed that because of this "show of good faith" it would be much more likely that the one who conceded would be given a "weighted vote" the next time a disagreement came up that seemed to have no obvious middle ground. This leads to my third suggestion.

3. When a solution requires one of you to change, try to determine which one will have an easier time changing on this issue.

I have found in my own marriage that there are some issues that I just have a harder time letting go of than others. The same is true for my wife. We've been married long enough to know which one of us is going to have an easier time changing, depending on the issue. Out of love for each other, we have to work together and agree that if it is important for one of us to make a change, it will likely be easier for one of us than the other, depending on the situation. Michael and Laura can help me illustrate this point.

Laura is a self-avowed perfectionist. She reminds me of Bree on the television show *Desperate Housewives*. Though I've never been to their home, I envision a sterile environment with everything perfectly placed. Michael is . . . well . . . not a perfectionist. Left to his own, things could get a little messy around the house. Surprisingly, their difference in this area causes little conflict in their relationship. The primary reason it doesn't is that Michael and Laura realize that one of them is going to have an easier time changing on this issue and have thus agreed to do so. Both of them accept that there's little hope of turning Laura into a laid-back, "let the clothes fall where they may" kind of personality. Michael, on the other hand, realizes that it's really not that big of a deal to put his underwear in the hamper rather than on the door handle or his dishes in the dishwasher instead of on the end table by the couch. As Michael has made some behavioral changes to "tidy up" for Laura, she has grown closer to him, knowing that he is doing this as an unselfish act of love because it's important to *her*.

I know what you Michaels out there are thinking: *Hey wait— that's not fair! Why can't Laura just lighten up and not be so rigid? Why does Michael have to do all the changing?* Well, you are right, it's not exactly what I'd call "fair," but in most mature, healthy marriages, a couple doesn't keep a scorecard and expect every interaction to be fair. In fact, the people in families who are most concerned with what's fair are kids between the ages of six and ten years old, and we all know how well *they* get along! The truth is, it would have worked just as well for Laura to relax her standards and just step over Michael's socks in the middle of the bedroom floor, or even pick them up herself. However, in *their* case, it was clearly easier for Michael to move toward her on this issue, and they both knew it. Because Michael was willing to do this, the issue is not really a big bone of contention between them anymore. Additionally, Laura sees Michael's efforts as a tangible expression of love. This endears him to her even more than ever, and it makes it easier to cut him some slack in other areas. Each couple needs to figure out which one will have an easier time changing when they encounter an issue that's particularly challenging and for which there's no way to make a compromise that will feel "fair."

4. Avoid the Four Horsemen when you discuss problems.

Again, Dr. Gottman's research is pretty clear that couples who regularly use criticism, defensiveness, stonewalling, and contempt in their arguments have much worse outcomes. I tell couples with whom I work that avoiding these Four Horsemen does require some self-discipline; however, I remind them that they use self-discipline already. For example, most couples (hopefully *all* couples) would never think of indulging their anger by physically striking their spouse (though most would agree that they've *felt* like it a time or two). It is just something that they have decided they will not do, no matter how angry or hurt they feel. It is important to put these Four Horsemen in the same category—just decide that no matter how hurt or angry you feel, such tactics are not an option for you.

5. Stay away from the following myth: "If I can present my case effectively, my spouse will have no choice other than to see the logic and truth of my argument and agree with me or give in."

Let me strongly encourage you to abandon belief in this myth. It will get you into big trouble. I have seen hundreds of couples in my office. Among those couples have been some exceptionally intelligent and articulate individuals. I honestly don't think I have ever witnessed a person engaged in a heated argument with their spouse suddenly say, "You know, when you put it that way, I guess I really can't argue with your logic. You are obviously right, and I'm wrong. How could I have not seen it all along?" One reason for this is because there are few issues about which couples argue where such a clear right or wrong can be easily found. It's pretty easy to defend either position and really believe in the cause. Second, whatever a couple is arguing about on the surface is usually connected to many other issues that often go far back into the history of their relationship. An argument between Jane and Jeff about why Jeff leaves the toilet seat up can really be connected in some way to Jane's anger about why he didn't stand up to his mother, who said Jane was selfish for wanting crab cakes at the wedding reception, since she knew that Jeff's mother doesn't like crab cakes. Finally, the emotions stirred by marital conflict are a deep and powerful river—sound logic and rational, well-made points won't always stop the flow. When a couple stops trying to win by making their point more "right," a much more productive problem-solving process can follow.

It is very important that in any disagreement or conflict, you are absolutely honest with yourself about any agenda you have to convert your spouse to your way of thinking. If you continue to address areas of conflict while secretly trying to convert your spouse to your way of thinking, you will never get to the task of discussing and resolving differences in a healthy, satisfactory, and effective manner.

6. Never, ever threaten divorce.

I tell all couples with whom I work that threatening divorce is a very destructive behavior that has disastrous effects. I consider threatening a spouse with divorce like pulling the fire alarm in a crowded theater—don't do it unless you mean it. Too often, I see couples who use this as a way to say, "I'm really angry at you right now." When I confront them about threatening divorce, they sometimes reply, "He knows I didn't really mean it." I say it doesn't matter—once you introduce the concept that divorce is an option, it sort of hangs there like an unverified spot on an X-ray: the possibility of what it could mean is just too anxiety producing. Both people in a marriage need to believe that the commitment to the relationship is paramount. The thought that divorce is a realistic option for one of them threatens the safety and stability of the relationship. It makes it difficult to do the hard work if things feel unstable and unsafe. Just make the commitment that divorce isn't a threat that you will use in your marriage. If you really believe that there are some issues that give you grounds for considering divorce (e.g., your spouse refuses to end an extramarital affair), then certainly make it clear that this issue is a "deal breaker" and address it as such. However, using the threat of divorce for issues that are not deal breakers can become a self-fulfilling prophecy.

7. Have some ground rules for discussing conflict.

In other words, you both need to agree that there are some rules that you will follow when you have inevitable disagreements and discussions about issues. You can make up your own list, but a sample list may include:

- It is okay to bring up any issue as long as we do not attack each other personally.
- We will always allow the other person to bring up an issue without becoming defensive. In fact, we will see this as a sign that the marriage is healthy. Apathetic people do not raise issues; only people who care bring up issues.
- We will agree that a problem for one of us is a problem for both of us. It is important to see ourselves as on the same team. It should be win-win or lose-lose.
- We will actively look for compromises rather than fighting for our positions or trying to be "right."
- If we cannot find a compromise after looking hard for one, we will try to assess whether one person feels more strongly about the issue than the other. If that is the case, we will agree to try to concede to that person. If we both feel equally strong about the issue, we will try to honestly determine which one of us will have an easier time changing on *this* issue. If there is no difference in how strongly each of us feels about it, or if we both feel that it will be difficult to

change, we will agree that we cannot find a solution right now, but will keep talking about it to see if we can find a solution or compromise later. We will remember that the most important thing is not that we find a solution, but that we can *talk about it safely with one another.*

8. Lead with the more "vulnerable" emotion first.

Most situations or issues that cause conflict are layered with many different emotions. Consider Marsha and Rick as an example. By the time they came to see me, they had been married seven years. They had two children: Chase, who was six years old, and little Ellen who was only fourteen months old. Chase was a difficult child. He was colicky as an infant, and this developed into frequent and intense temper tantrums as a toddler. Chase's "meltdowns" were getting worse, and he was under the care of a child psychiatrist for these issues. When Ellen came along, the family system was overwhelmed. Marsha had her hands full with Chase when he was an only child. However, with the demands of a new baby, Marsha felt completely overwhelmed. Rick was a faithful husband and a good provider. He understood and agreed about the severity of Chase's issues. However, he felt that whatever he did to try to help was never quite enough to make Marsha feel supported.

Marsha's anger was almost tangible as she sat on the sofa in my office with her arms tightly folded across her chest. She sat rigidly with a scowl on her face. Every muscle in her body seemed tense. It took only one simple question from me to open the floodgates and hear what she was so furious about—"So Marsha, you seem upset; what's going on?" At that invitation, Marsha began to pour out what seemed like months of anger and resentment. "I just don't know how much more I can take. Chase is getting worse rather than better, and Rick doesn't get it. He thinks as long as he works and brings home the money, he's done his part. I'm left here all day to handle this little tyrant, and then Rick has the nerve to think I want to have sex when he gets home. Is he just clueless or what?"

After some discussion, I was able to help Marsha understand that her anger was really only one of many emotions that were causing her to feel so overwhelmed. If she looked behind this wall of rage, she would discover that there were many other emotions she was experiencing. For example, she was feeling anxious and scared because she didn't see how she would be able to deal with Chase if he continued to have these outbursts. Marsha was accustomed to effectively dealing with difficult situations in her life, and this was perhaps the first time that she felt she was up against a challenge that she might not be able to handle. She also loved Chase, but she was starting to feel very angry at him because of the chaos he was creating in the family. She resented the fact that she couldn't commit as much time and energy to Ellen because Chase was so demanding and high-maintenance. Some of her thoughts about Chase were so negative; she was feeling guilty that she could actually have such negative thoughts and feelings about her own son. In addition to all of these painful and difficult emotions, Marsha was actually jealous of her friends who seemed to have an easier time with their kids. Her best friend Sharon also had two children, but neither of them had any specific issues or needs that made parenting a challenge. Sharon seemed to just breeze through the day without much difficulty. Marsha felt "cheated" because of her situation.

I explained to Marsha that some painful emotions cause us to feel more vulnerable than others. For example, when one feels anxious and scared, it feels much more powerless and helpless than when one feels angry. In my experience, it is often easier to experience anger than other feelings such as fear, guilt, or jealousy. When I feel angry, I feel less vulnerable. Anger is often empowering and is accompanied by many fewer feelings of vulnerability than many of the other emotions that can be elicited by marital conflict. I often see couples become very angry toward each other when one or both of them feel frightened that one of them is distancing from the other. The more honest (but more vulnerable) emotion associated with this experience is fear and sadness. However, it feels much more vulnerable to say to your spouse, "I'm feeling very sad and anxious because you seem so far away," than to act out in anger or express these feelings verbally in an angry way such as, "You're so selfish. You never spend any time with me!"

The difference is important, because the emotion you express and the way you express it usually dictates the response you receive from your spouse. Most people react to anger by becoming defensive (remember the Four Horsemen?) rather than supportive and engaging. An angry response typically does not result in getting needs met or having your spouse respond favorably to a complaint or a request. Leading with the more vulnerable emotion, however, often elicits a much less defensive response and is much more likely to be met with a favorable response to a request or a complaint.

9. When you feel angry at your spouse, ask yourself, "What do I want from my spouse right now?" and then try to turn your anger into a request.

I have found that when one person is angry at his spouse over something, that anger is often a secondary emotion. This means that the anger this person feels is really an emotion that springs from a different primary emotion such as disappointment, fear, or loneliness, among others. As I discussed earlier, anger is simply an easier emotion to express and causes us to feel less vulnerable. Too often a person waits until he is angry to approach his spouse and then a harsh start-up (as opposed to Gottman's suggestion of a soft start-up for conflict) results in an attack-defend dynamic between the couple. I encourage people to stop when they are angry and engage in some self-examination. Try to understand where your anger is coming from. Ask yourself questions such as, "What did my spouse do or fail to do that is causing me to feel so angry?" "What feeling other than anger does this cause me to have?" "What do I really want to request from my spouse right now?"

Ray was furious at Amy because she forgot to take his laundry to the cleaners. When he went to the closet to get the dress shirt that he planned to wear for his presentation and discovered that it was dirty, he exploded. His attack on Amy caused her to shut down emotionally, and when they came in to my office, they had barely spoken for days. I encouraged Ray to move past his anger to articulate what he felt (other than anger) when he discovered that Amy had forgotten to drop the laundry off at the cleaners. With some effort, Ray acknowledged that he felt disappointed, hurt, and more than anything, uncared for. I encouraged Ray to stay with those feelings and to calmly and rationally explain his feelings to Amy without attacking her. During this conversation, Ray also talked about how he had been feeling ignored for months since the baby arrived and that he was actually growing resentful because he felt that Amy rarely even thought of him much anymore. Amy was surprised to hear how Ray had been feeling. She acknowledged that she had been feeling overwhelmed, and that she probably did pay less attention to Ray. The dirty shirt was simply a "last straw" for Ray, and he admitted that he really overreacted by getting so angry. Ray was able to make a simple request from Amy, "I would like to have more of your attention." Amy validated his need to have more attention while admitting that she was feeling overwhelmed. After feeling that his needs were legitimate and gaining a greater understanding of why Amy was more preoccupied and less attentive to him, his anger virtually went away, and he was much more understanding and patient with Amy.

10. Make sure your requests are not presented as demands.

Everyone has things they would like to ask from their spouse. The list is endless and can include everything from a major request (e.g., I want my mother to move in with us; I want to have another child; I want to move to Kenya) to a moderate request (I want you to start going to church with me; I want to have sex more often; I want you to lose weight) to a minor request (I want you to stop holding your fork that way; I want you to pick up my dry cleaning). What one person considers a minor request may be considered moderate or even major by the other. Being married means making and receiving requests almost constantly.

I see couples get into all kinds of trouble when they turn requests into expectations or worse—demands. Pastor and author Andy Stanley says couples make a major mistake when "I do" becomes a magic phrase that transforms desires into expectations. For example, a man may marry a woman *hoping* that he will walk in the door every night to a home-cooked meal served by a vixen in high heels. Or a woman may marry a man *desiring* to live in a five-bedroom estate on a lake, with a guest house where the live-in nanny cooks dinner every night. There's nothing wrong with dreams, hopes, and desires. However, when these become things we expect in a marriage, look out. This is obviously a big topic, and I firmly believe that any and all expectations should be fully disclosed and discussed prior to the trip down the aisle. However, even if expectations are managed and kept to a minimum, there will still be lots of requests within a relationship. Some requests are harder to hear than others. Take Ben and Tara for example.

Ben and Tara made a handsome young couple with lots going for them. They had a healthy new baby, Ben had a successful career, and Tara was also a successful physician. They had successfully worked out a schedule that allowed both of them to take care of Luke, and their teamwork was impressive. Before Luke was born, Ben and Tara were active and enjoyed lots of recreational activities together. They loved to hike, bike ride, and go to the gym together. Before Tara became pregnant, Ben and Tara were in great physical shape—trim and lean. Tara gained the expected pregnancy weight, and she was determined to get back into shape after her pregnancy. Soon after Luke was born, Tara's borderline obsession with working out shifted to her role as a new mother. She now felt the pressure to devote enough time and energy to her career while also being a good mother to Luke. She no longer felt motivated to spend ninety minutes every day at the gym, and her concern about "good carbs," glycemic indexes, and other aspects of health waned considerably.

By the time Luke was two years old, Tara was even heavier than when she delivered. Ben, on the other hand, continued to work out as faithfully as ever. In fact, he was training for a marathon by the time they came to see me. This was a source of conflict as it required him to be absent from the home more frequently on training runs. During one session, Ben awkwardly shared that he was no longer attracted to Tara. He admitted that he felt shallow, and that her weight shouldn't really matter. However, he felt he could no longer pretend that Tara's weight was not an issue for him. This revelation hurt Tara; but to her credit, she did not hear it as a rejection of her as a person. She was as unsatisfied with her appearance as Ben was, and she acknowledged that she had really let herself go physically. They were able to discuss the issue, albeit uncomfortably, and Ben made a request that Tara could respond to.

The rule in my practice is that any request in a marriage is fair as long as it is not connected to one of three things: (1) your love for your spouse, (2) your acceptance of your spouse as a person (which differs from acceptance of unacceptable or inappropriate behavior), and (3) your commitment to your spouse. These three (the "holy trinity" of the marriage) are nonconditional. They are part of your marital vows to your spouse and do not change, even if desires are not always met. These three are free gifts that do not have to be earned. Many couples get into trouble when they feel that their partner's love, acceptance, or commitment may be withdrawn or withheld if requests are not met. If you threaten to withdraw or withhold any or all of these three, you are being manipulative and unfair. Make your requests, but disconnect them from one of these three things. I agree with Willard Harley, who calls "selfish demands" one of the "love busters" in a marriage. He agrees that making requests is part of any relationship but that turning these requests into demands (i.e., expectations) because of one person's selfish desires does not work.

In order to be clear, I would not want anyone to believe that I am saying, "I don't have to do anything if I don't want to because you can't make demands of me." I believe that part of being married means that each person makes a commitment to invest 100 percent into the relationship and to make individual sacrifices out of love for one's spouse. If you are serious about being married, you do everything you can to attend to and fulfill your spouse's needs and desires. What I caution against, however, is using manipulation and threats or using power plays to get your spouse to yield to a demand. If your spouse feels that one of your demands is unreasonable, then you both need to go back to the previous sections on how to communicate and look for solutions to disagreements that you can both agree on.

Finally, your response to your spouse's requests should be considered a gift of love rather than a response to a demand or threat. Tara willingly agreed to Ben's request to lose weight. However, she did so as an act of love to Ben. Had she felt forced to lose weight in order to keep his love, acceptance, or commitment, the response would have been doomed to fail even if she had lost the weight, because it would have resulted in feelings of resentment and insecurity. It helped Tara when she realized over a long weekend that she was less attracted to Ben after he took a break from shaving for a few days. She acknowledged that while her feelings for him were still the same, she just wasn't as attracted to him with a face full of stubble. This helped Tara understand how Ben's level of attraction did not reflect his feelings of love for her. Make sure that your responses to your spouse's requests are acts of love rather than responses to demands. Should you decide that you cannot respond favorably to your spouse's request, resist belittling or invalidating the request. Instead, state honestly and clearly why you feel unable to respond and engage in a discussion about how the two of you can work together to reach a resolution.

11. Work to stay connected to each other on a daily basis.

The research shows that all of us have a tendency to let our feelings about our spouses influence our interactions with them. Our most recent feelings about our spouse act as a filter through which we interpret their words and actions. For example, if I am feeling particularly close to my wife, I am likely to have a preponderance of positive feelings about her. This will lead to a more positive filter and cause me to give her the benefit of the doubt more often, to hear her complaints more readily, and to want to work harder to meet her in the middle.

When I am feeling disconnected from her, those positive feelings may be in short supply, and my filter changes to a more negative one. Consequently, I am less likely to consider her side of things, I may take a more stubborn and defensive posture in disagreements, and I may assign more malicious motives and intents to her actions. It is vital that you work to stay connected with each other in order to let those positive feelings influence your interactions with each other. Staying connected will require more effort after you bring a new baby into the house. However, the effort pays off well. Here are a few tips:

- Hug or kiss each other hello and goodbye. It is surprising how many couples stop doing this after a while.
- Remember your manners with your spouse. "Please," "thank you," and "excuse me" aren't just for strangers or business associates—these cordialities go a long way in marriages too.
- Smile at each other.
- Take walks together.
- Hold hands more often.
- Share details from your day with each other. Don't just talk about what is "newsworthy."
- "Gossip" with each other. I realize that this is a strange recommendation; however, sharing "secrets" with one another and trusting one person with your private thoughts seems to strengthen the friendship bond with your spouse.

- Look for a way to do something thoughtful for your spouse at least once a day (e.g., make a cup of tea, give a two-minute shoulder massage, turn down the bed, leave a note, etc.)
- Compliment your spouse at least once daily.
- Pray and worship together.

And so . . .

Conflict in a marriage is not bad—in fact the absence of conflict is often worse (it often signals apathy). Begin to see conflict and problems in your marriage like any other chore that you don't like but accept as an inevitable part of life (e.g., laundry, dishes, taking out the trash, mowing the yard). Understand that the way you talk about problems is more important than the solutions you come up with. Change the way you talk about problems in your relationship. Stay connected with each other because this will influence how you talk to and treat each other when problems come up.

3

Feeling the Pressure

Handling Increased Responsibility

Homecoming

Few memories in my life are as vivid as the day Dana and I brought Caleb home from the hospital. It was Saturday, December 10, 1994. It was a typical winter day in Atlanta, Georgia—the sky was gray and the air was damp and cool. I remember walking to the parking lot and driving the car to the area of the hospital where Dana and Caleb would be brought down via wheelchair by the nurse. Caleb was bundled tightly in his receiving blanket, wearing the knit cap the hospital provided. I helped Dana place Caleb into the car seat for the first time. We checked and double-checked to make sure he was secure and that we had placed everything where it was supposed to go. I then loaded our things into the car and began the short drive to our house.

Moments after we pulled away from the hospital, Caleb began crying (actually, it was more of a soul-piercing shriek) in what we would later learn was his normal mode of communication. At the time, however, it elicited panic from me and especially Dana. The maternal urge was to "make him better." I struggled between driving ultracautiously and rushing to get home, as though by some instinct Caleb would "recognize" that he was home and feel comforted and secure. When we did arrive home, we hurriedly took Caleb inside and Dana immediately tried to breastfeed him and quiet his state of discontentment. After a few more minutes of rocking, he settled down, fell asleep, and she placed him in the bassinet. I still remember standing in our den, the sight of the Christmas tree, the smell of the house, and the red shirt that Dana was wearing. I looked at her as she sat in the rocking chair beside Caleb, and she stared back at me like the proverbial deer in the headlights.

Though neither of us said a word, it was clear that we were both thinking, *Dear God, what are we supposed to do now?* The only image I can think of to describe how both of us were feeling at that moment is when Wile E. Coyote looks up to see a huge boulder falling on his head. The sudden realization that we were now *responsible* for this precious, innocent, and completely helpless infant was absolutely overwhelming. Dana started to cry, and I remember thinking, *Wait, this is the day I have been anticipating for just over nine months. This is supposed to be the happiest day of our life.* I was a little disillusioned. I later learned that Dana was not crying out of sadness, but out of a feeling of being overwhelmed with the feeling of ultimate responsibility.

Don't misunderstand; we were both thrilled at having our son home with us. I cannot imagine any couple being more eager for a baby to arrive than we were prior to his birth. We were not, however, prepared for the feeling of responsibility that accompanied his homecoming.

Even bright, well-educated, and well-prepared parents can be overwhelmed with the responsibilities of parenting. There are excellent books on every topic of child-care, and I recommend that expectant and new parents read to prepare. Unfortunately, nothing can prepare new parents for the instinctive emotional and even visceral response that is elicited by their infant's expression of his needs. A hungry infant's cry can rouse a sleep-deprived mother from REM sleep in milliseconds. A baby with gas can cause two adults to scramble in a fashion that makes a Chinese fire drill look like Olympic synchronized swimming. When an infant is in distress, parents mobilize. There is an instinctive "fight or flight" response that sends neurotransmitters freely flowing. To an objective observer, the reaction is often comical. To the parent, the response is automatic.

I once heard about a study of careers that placed workers at high risk for "stress." The researchers reported that air traffic controllers had a higher rate of some objective measures of stress (such as high blood pressure) than individuals in other types of jobs. They hypothesized that air traffic controllers are probably more "stressed" than others because they are in a constant state of hypervigilance. In other words, they were constantly scanning the screen to avert potential disaster. One mistake could result in catastrophe. New parents often maintain this state of hypervigilance. I have had couples tell me that they haven't slept in weeks, even during times when their infant is sleeping soundly. When questioned, many tell me that they have the baby monitor on in their bedroom and that they wake constantly at the slightest noise (or sometimes lack of any noise—causing them to conclude that their baby has stopped breathing). This constant state of hyperarousal and vigilance is stressful and demanding. New parents often maintain a readiness to act that prevents them from ever feeling that they can completely relax or focus their attention on anything other than their baby.

While this state of alertness is demanding for any length of time, it is often unrelenting, especially for new mothers. This is particularly true for those new mothers who breastfeed their babies. Many new mothers describe to me that they feel that they are always "on call." In many ways, they are. An infant lacks any ability to delay gratification. They are little beings who respond instinctively and immediately to any and every need. Usually this expression is in the form of crying—not just normal crying, but really loud and intense crying. Babies don't keep schedules well, either. Thus, in the early months, there is an intensity of needs that is constant. Maintaining this readiness to act for twenty-four hours a day, seven days a week is exhausting, to say the least. This combination of intensity + consistency = depletion. New parents describe feeling depleted both physically and emotionally.

Soon after your baby becomes mobile, you learn that babies have a natural proclivity toward seeking out the most hazardous area of a room or house. Objects that look innocent and harmless find new ways to pose a threat in the hands of a crawler. The first time a parent sees his infant chewing on the lamp cord or about to insert the small object she just found behind the couch into her mouth can cause even the calmest parent to become frantic. Even the most thorough parents who have taken an inventory of their home to eliminate the potential dangers find that they have not anticipated every possible threat. The anxiety caused by the realization of household hazards is only compounded by the horrors waiting outside the confines of home. Even rational and logical parents can reach anxiety levels of paranoid proportions. Parents can think anyone who has not been to their house for dinner and completed an FBI background check is a potential pedophile, and a chance encounter with the wrong person could result in a fatal case of bird flu. For the parent, there is an ever-present feeling of the need to protect the child from every possible risk. This too, takes an enormous psychological toll on the parents.

If this is your first baby, let me forewarn you that most new parents often succumb to the need to measure their child's development against every other baby they have ever heard of or read about. If you have friends with babies, you may be tempted to ask when they started to sleep through the night, sat up alone, started crawling, walking, talking, and all the other things babies do. Try to resist the temptation! First of all, every baby progresses at different rates of development. The word *normal* is relative when it comes to childhood development. Professionals use the term *within normal limits* to indicate a wide range of time within which it is considered normal for a child to reach a certain developmental milestone. This time frame is typically within a period of several months. Don't worry if your friend's baby of the same age started walking several months ago and yours is still crawling. If you are seeing your pediatrician at the scheduled times, he or she will let you know if you have anything to be concerned about.

In addition, let me forewarn you about stories from parents of older children. For some reason, parents tend either to forget or to exaggerate their child's development. There are many suburban legends out there of a two-year-old who was reading the *New York Times* and was fully potty-trained by four months of age. When you hear about these wonder babies, resist the temptation to compare your "normal" child to these myths. Instead, simply smile and say, "How nice."

At some point early in the child-rearing experience, every parent is bound to discover his or her first lesson in powerlessness.

The parent is forced to confront the reality that at times there is nothing that he or she can do to please or satisfy a crying baby. Try as you may, you cannot eliminate every risk posed to your child. The fact is, you can be a good parent—even a really, really good parent. But you will never be a perfect parent. In my experience, the earlier this course in powerlessness is taken in life, the better for everyone. Your baby will get sick, and it may not be because dad forgot to put a hat on junior for the trip to the store. Your baby will likely have a few marathon crying spells that are not because you are a neglectful or inadequate parent. Many people have great difficulty with this concept of powerlessness.

The Impact on New Parents

How does all of this added responsibility affect a marriage? I see the added responsibility introduced into the home as having a direct impact on the marital relationship. Let me offer a few examples:

Physical Impact

Have you ever noticed how the man who assumes the office of president of the United States seems to age about twenty years during his four-year term as president? Some believe that this "accelerated aging" is a result of the stress associated with that level of responsibility. Have you ever noticed how much older a new parent looks after the first year of parenting? Coincidence? Maybe not. As mentioned previously, maintaining a constant vigil requires the body to summon a great deal of energy to remain alert and poised to act. This energy is finite and must be constantly replenished.

Fatigue and sleep deprivation have nasty consequences. For example, the brain requires sufficient sleep in order to properly refresh neurotransmitters such as serotonin, dopamine, and norepinephrine. When the process of making and properly restoring these brain chemicals is interfered with (as in a lack of sleep) over a period of time, the person is at greater risk of suffering depression and anxiety. In addition, we are simply unable to cope with stress as effectively when we are sleep deprived. Tempers are short and patience is low when we are not rested. In addition to a lack of rest and sleep, new parents often find that they no longer have time to exercise, which is too bad, because exercise is a great stress reducer. It is no wonder that new parents look and feel exhausted and depleted.

Relational Impact

Most parents siphon off other areas to conserve energy during this time. One of the chief areas from which energy is taken is the marriage. No more late night talks, watching TV, or reading in bed together. Gone are the long and quiet meals where you catch up with you spouse at the end of the day. You know you brought home the right baby from the hospital, but you begin to have this nagging suspicion that someone switched spouses on you. You went in with this fun, energetic, spontaneous partner. But now, you share your home with an irritable, tired, and unavailable person whom you barely recognize.

Additionally, because you are constantly in a "need-meeting" state with a newborn, it is easy to become resentful of your partner when he expresses even the most basic needs. The result is a partner who feels rejected and resentful because simple expressions of basic needs are often met with irritability or impatience. You know you are in trouble when you lose it after your spouse asks you to pass the salt at the dinner table!

Finally, the effect of this added responsibility on a marriage comes in the form of averted attentions. A newborn has a tremendous need for attention. New parents are always listening for the baby's expressed needs. Infants and toddlers are needy little beings. They almost constantly want something—from having a diaper changed, to wanting a pacifier or bottle, to just being picked up and noticed. Young children just aren't very self-sufficient. Prior to the child's birth, spouses may have directed much of this attention and energy toward each other. Attention from your spouse now is in the form of leftovers, and there aren't many of those at the end of an exhausting day.

Emotional Impact

There is also an emotional price to pay for this added responsibility. The stress of constantly being "on call" can have significant emotional side effects. There have been numerous studies that explore an individual's response to "stress." Such a discussion is far beyond the scope of this book. Suffice it to say that such long-standing stress can have varied effects depending on many factors (e.g., support and help available, an individual's personality type, the person's perception of the stress, and how much other stress the person is dealing with at the same time). Chemical changes take place in our bodies when we are experiencing stress such as a rise in cortisol levels (a specific type of steroid hormone the body produces in response to stress). It is not uncommon for a parent to struggle with feelings of irritability, sadness, and even depression secondary to prolonged stress. Some people respond to this kind of stress with coping methods that actually exacerbate the situation (e.g., alcohol abuse, overwork, tobacco use, etc.).

What to Do

I have some suggestions which may help buffer your life and your marriage from the felt effects of the added responsibility factor introduced by adding children to a family:

Now Where Did They Put That Owner's Manual?

New parents should give themselves permission to be novices. You cannot possibly know everything there is to know about parenting. Besides, it is my experience that most parental fears and worries are greatly magnified, and later seem rather small in retrospect. This is why seasoned parents seem so calm—they have learned from experience that few things are true emergencies. Obviously, it is okay to ask for advice and help when you need it, even if you simply need to hear it to make yourself feel better. Even the most prepared parents will find those occasional days when Murphy's Law (i.e., anything that can go wrong will go wrong) is in full force. It is important to have realistic expectations. Accept that there will be days when no matter what you do right, things will go wrong. The good news is that these days end and will likely be followed by good days. Keep your eyes and ears open for those priceless moments when your baby looks at you in the way that only *he* can and makes you realize that you never thought you could love someone this much. This kind of love is greater than all the mistakes you will ever make.

If you're worried that you might really make a mistake, don't worry—you will. Get over it. Many new parents act as though their baby is a china doll—make one wrong move and it's all over. Clearly, newborns are physically delicate and need to be handled with care. I'm not advocating taking risks with children. However, many new parents go beyond being "reasonably careful" to being virtually neurotic. This is especially true when it comes to eating. New parents, especially new mothers, can worry themselves sick if an infant isn't particularly hungry at one feeding. Don't panic. If you are getting regular health care checks for your baby from your pediatrician, he or she will let you know if you need to worry about whether your baby is adequately nourished and growing properly. Obviously, if your child is not eating at all, there is a problem. However, don't fear that your baby is going to starve if he is occasionally fussy at a meal.

One thing you also need to get comfortable with is the fact that newborns fuss and cry. They don't have any other way to communicate yet. Therefore, a fussy infant might be telling you she is hungry or needs a diaper change. However, she also may be telling you she is bored, tired, cranky, or that she is in some other state of unhappiness that doesn't require you to scramble to "fix" it. If you've checked the usual suspects (fever, diaper, etc.) and she is still fussy, you may need to let her fuss.

The other area where parents tend to become overanxious is regarding their child's emotional development. There seems to be a belief among parents (of children of all ages based on my experience) that parents generally mess their kids up psychologically, and we have to be really careful not to scar their fragile little psyches. As kids get older, this often results in parents failing to discipline their children properly or refusing to set appropriate limits for fear of damaging their child's self-esteem. Again, this is a topic that deserves a book on its own; however, let me assure you that kids are very psychologically resilient. Kids who grow up in a home with present and loving (not perfect) parents do fine. You'll make tons of mistakes, and your kids will forgive you and get over them with no lasting harm.

It has been said that today's parents may be the most insecure parents of any generation. I'm not sure I can list all the factors that contribute to this phenomenon, but I do see a great deal of self-doubt, particularly among first-time parents. Try to relax: the things your new baby needs most are the things you will probably give instinctively. Besides the basics of food, clothing, and shelter, they need affection, love, and human interaction. Also, make sure they don't stick a fork in an electrical outlet. The rest is just gravy.

Take Charge

Establish a home environment that feels in control. For newborns, this means that you learn to distinguish and respond differently to your baby's cries. If your baby is fussing "normally," resist the urge to respond as though it were a 911 call. For older children, establish clear and reasonable limits and enforce them consistently. Try to establish some routines as a family. Structure often helps to calm an otherwise chaotic environment. Strive to gather for meals as often as possible. Turn off "noise" in your home whenever possible (e.g., radios, TVs, computers). The need to eliminate noise is especially true at mealtimes. Invest some time and money in getting your home organized. An organized environment can create more of a feeling of being in control as opposed to out of control.

I realize that people are scattered all over the continuum of organizational skills. Some people are just naturally good at order and organization while others would consider it a major accomplishment to get the bed made. Despite the differences among people, almost everyone seems to function better and feel less out of control in an environment that is not chaotic. For perfectionists, it will be frustrating that you won't be able to maintain your home like you could before you invited a newborn to live there. For those of you who are naturally disorganized, a newborn may move you from chaos to catastrophe. My advice is to work on the major areas of your home and try to keep them from becoming out of control. A mother once told me that if she just concentrated on her kitchen, everything else seemed to work out. She felt that the kitchen was the nerve center of the house, and that as the kitchen goes, so goes the rest of the house. I think she was on to something.

To Care Is to Share

Share being "on call." It is important for each parent to feel that there is some time to relax without keeping an ear open for a crying baby. Sometimes simply knowing that the other parent will be responding to the child during the night can mean a sound night's sleep. It is typical for mom to take at least some time off after giving birth and for dad to go back to work very soon. In this arrangement, mom usually does "night duty" since dad has to get up and go to work. I'll say more about this later, but I would suggest that at the very least, dad needs to take at least one weekend night so mom can get a full night's sleep. An even better arrangement, if possible, would be for dad to arrange to go in late on a Wednesday or Thursday so he can do night feedings and let mom look forward to a full night's sleep during the week. Constantly interrupted sleep over a prolonged period of time (even if that person is getting short naps during the day) is a recipe for many bad things (irritability, fatigue, even depression and anxiety).

In the early stages, it often works well for one parent to take over and let the other go to a movie, a quiet dinner, shopping, or simply for a long drive to get away. This time is vital for replenishing. Try to share the daily tasks as well. This is especially important if mom is home with the baby while dad is at work. For me, taking over the nighttime rituals (bathing, brushing teeth, reading stories, etc.) was a wonderful time of bonding for me, Caleb, and Benjamin. It also gave Dana a chance to have a few moments to herself in the evening. Fathers will enjoy and experience the role of fatherhood sooner if they can take over some of the daily routine with the new baby. This team approach will also help spread the feeling of responsibility. It feels much less overwhelming realizing that you have a partner to help you. I have more to say about dad's role of helping in the chapter for dads.

Dating—The Lost Art

I haven't discovered why people forget how to date when they get married and have children. When you feel ready to leave your baby with a qualified sitter or family member, try to find some time to go out with each other. You must be proactive about this. If you wait for a convenient time, it simply will not happen. You need to plan and schedule dates. I'm really serious about this—if you don't plan and schedule it, it probably won't happen. This also gives you something to look forward to which has a positive psychological effect as well. There is actually a great deal of benefit derived from the anticipation of enjoying an activity in addition to the event itself. Just think about how much fun it is counting down the days until Christmas or a long-overdue vacation. Traditional wisdom for couples used to include a recommendation that parents make a rule to not discuss the children when on dates. However, recent research of happy couples indicates that they do talk about the children. Of course, it's certainly fine to talk about other topics, but don't feel like you can't talk about the children while you are on a date. After all, your children are now a major part of your life. It would be foolish to pretend otherwise. The point is to *connect with each other*.

The feeling of responsibility for parenting is difficult to escape when you are at home. You and your spouse need to get away occasionally for an evening and really connect with one another—even if you are connecting by talking about the baby and your role as new parents. Recall the data that revealed the importance of having a friendship at the core of a happy marriage. You and your spouse are growing and changing. Consequently, you need to stay connected with each other by having time to share adult conversation and to enjoy one another's company. You dated before you married your spouse in order to get to know this wonderful person better. Perhaps it is a good idea to continue dating after you are married to make sure you continue to know each other better.

Now that you are parents, you aren't the same people you were before. You see the world differently, and in all likelihood, your dreams, goals, and priorities are changing as well. You should learn how these things are changing in your spouse. It's like dating all over again, and it can be just as fun! It is also vital because research on marriage indicates that in the happiest marriages, each person sees their spouse as supportive of their dreams, goals, and aspirations. Dr. Gottman's research also shows that the happiest couples create a shared vision for their lives. In other words, they form a vision or mission statement regarding what their life together is about, and they see each other as the coauthor of that vision.

Many new parents are reluctant to leave their newborn with a sitter and go out for an evening together, particularly in the early stages. My wife and I laugh now about our first date after our first son was born. We got a sitter and went out for a movie—not a big deal. I purchased my normal bag of popcorn and large Diet Coke and settled in to enjoy a movie. I don't remember which movie we saw, but I do recall that as soon as the movie was over, I was ready to find the men's room. (Did I mention that it was a *large* Diet Coke?) My wife, however, had other ideas. She grabbed my hand and pulled me toward the parking lot with a firm, "You can go at home!" In the car, I inquired about the emergency and discovered that we had reached the threshold of her anxiety regarding leaving Caleb alone with a sitter for the first time. (Do you know just *how* large those movie Cokes are?)

She laughs about this now and sees how overly anxious she was at the time. However, at this stage, we had reached outside her comfort zone too quickly. As our son got a little older, we grew more comfortable with sitters and were even able to catch dinner *and* a movie—with a bathroom stop included. We just needed time to get there. (I still get a little nervous when I see those great big drink cups in the theater, though.)

Occasionally, try to double-date or go out with other couples. I have found that all of us act a little differently around adults other than our spouses (unfortunately, we are often better behaved!) It's good to experience your spouse interacting with other adults. It offers you a view of and experience of your spouse that you don't get to see often. Furthermore, there are aspects of your spouse that are very attractive and appealing to you that are more clearly manifest in these types of situations. For example, Jim had long lamented that he felt that his wife did not really respect him. She focused on what she saw as his inadequacies at home. For example, he wasn't exactly the handiest guy on the street. A broken cabinet door could stay broken for months, and when he did try to fix it, there was a very good chance that he would drop the hammer on the hardwood floor, causing a dent, and he would likely bang the level into the wall requiring a paint touch-up.

This drove Sandra crazy. Her father was Mr. Fix-It, and she just couldn't understand how a man could be so helpless and useless around the house. Jim acknowledged that he wasn't very good around the house. His solution was to hire a handyman for these things, but Sandra could not let go of the belief that Jim "should be able to do it." As simple and relatively benign as this issue sounds, it worried me as their therapist because I also knew that Jim was an incredibly talented attorney. He was almost revered in his profession, and he received a ton of accolades and admiration from those who worked with him. I used the term "worried" because I knew that if Jim continued to be showered with respect, admiration, and praise from his colleagues while being criticized and belittled at home, it would just be a matter of time before he'd start finding reasons to stay at work later and later.

A significant shift occurred one weekend when Jim and Sandra took a brief vacation with two other couples. Sandra observed how Jim interacted with the other adults on the trip. She stated to me in an individual session, "I have to admit, I saw Jim in a different light on this trip. He really is one of the smartest people I know. The other people were asking him questions, and I was amazed at how wise and thoughtful he is. I found myself feeling about him like I did when we were first dating. I suppose I caught a glimpse of what everyone else sees in him at his job. He's a pretty amazing guy. I guess he doesn't have as much of a chance to show this side of himself at home." While this may be a dramatic example, it is not uncommon for us to see different characteristics of our spouse that are not readily apparent to us in the course of day-to-day life when given a chance to interact with other adults.

Stressbusting

There are many wonderful ways to reduce the added stress of parenting. Things like muscle relaxation, hot baths, afternoon teas, walks, or getting out to have a manicure or drive some golf balls are invaluable and effective stress busters. Proper diet and nutrition is also a buffer from stress. Exercise is important too, even if in limited amounts. If possible, spouses should help each other relax. For example, offer to wash your spouse's hair one night, give a back rub or foot massage, read to each other, or have tea together (preferably decaffeinated). One important technique of stress management is to learn the signs and symptoms your body gives to let you know that you are in need of some stress reduction. This varies among individuals, but look for irritability, sadness, physical complaints (e.g., weakness, muscle tension, headaches, etc.), picking up bad habits, restlessness, worry, or other symptoms of stress. When the signs appear, take action.

Priorities

Especially during the early months of bringing a new baby into your home, you will likely have to accept that you cannot accomplish the same things you did before your baby arrived. Agree with your spouse which tasks need to be redistributed (more about this in the next chapter), and which simply need to be left alone for now. An unmade bed or clothes on the floor will not matter in a few months. Your neighbors will understand if your lawn is not perfect this spring. (Note: This is a particularly difficult challenge for those of you on the more compulsive end of the continuum. I speak from experience.) Establishing unrealistic goals will lead to increased stress and feelings of being overwhelmed. Read *Don't Sweat the Small Stuff* by Richard Carlson to help you with prioritizing. As I said earlier, avoid allowing your home to reach a state of chaos, as this will increase your feelings of stress. However, you need to abandon the quest for perfection.

The Big Picture

You've heard everyone say to you, "Enjoy it now, they grow up so fast." When you are in these intense early years of child rearing, you might paraphrase this as, "Don't worry, you won't be this stressed out too much longer." The incredible responsibility you both feel now is indeed a brief stage. As you both begin to feel more skilled at caring for your new baby, you will feel less pressure. Additionally, you will find that your baby does develop quickly and will not be so completely dependent upon you for his or her every need for very long. Someone very wise once said, "The days are long, but the years are short." That statement sums it up pretty well. Try to keep perspective and enjoy each stage of your child's development without getting overwhelmed by the feelings of responsibility.

Simplify

Refuse to believe that your child must be involved in every activity in order to enjoy maximum developmental benefit. The children I see who are the most stressed and anxious are the ones that have a schedule as busy as a moonlighting medical resident. Children need downtime. So do parents. While most so-called enrichment opportunities are fine, they are hardly *necessary* for your child to develop and reach his full potential. Unfortunately, I encounter too many parents that have fallen prey to good marketing and feel they are being neglectful in their responsibilities as a good parent if their child is not involved in all types of extracurricular events or programs. I've talked with too many parents who seem to believe that their children need to be able to play the cello and read the classics before they start first grade. This is utter nonsense.

To be honest, for at least the first six years (and probably beyond), many programs that purport to give children a head start are not much more than expensive babysitting opportunities. I think that it is just as healthy (and certainly cheaper) to take toddlers to a McDonald's playground and let them loose for an hour or so while you watch. They'll love it, and it's good for them. Relax and have a cup of coffee while your youngster romps in the plastic ball pit.

Simplify your "family time" as well. The importance of early parent-child bonding is well established in the research literature. Keep in mind that this type of bonding can take place more effectively in your backyard than it can at Disney World. Many parents mistakenly believe the commercials that suggest family bonding takes place at amusement parks or other expensive venues. In reality, these settings can offer so many distractions that personal interaction can be minimal. The best type of family interactions can take place at a kitchen table over a board game, in the backyard while kicking a soccer ball around, or on a hike. The main thing is to spend focused time and attention on one another—not the setting.

Lean on Me

Regardless of your child's age, remember that you have a partner in parenting. Share your feelings with your partner. When you begin to feel overwhelmed, talk with your spouse and ask for support and for help. One of the biggest reasons people feel disappointed with or resentful of their spouse is simply because they fail to make specific requests. Don't be too proud to say, "Honey, I'm feeling overwhelmed and need for you to help me find a way to calm down." You have not because you ask not.

Parenting does increase the responsibility level in your life. It is a challenge to take on this extra responsibility and maintain the investment needed to nurture a solid marital relationship. I hope you will use some of these suggestions to help you find the balance. I also encourage you to discuss other ways to do this that I may not have mentioned. I have found that the best ideas often come from couples who know each other and devise solutions that are uniquely effective for them.

4

Dividing the Chores

Who Does What Now?

There are lots of things that new parents can argue and fight about once the baby comes home from the hospital. The topics include things nonparent couples battle over, such as sex, money, and in-law issues. They also include issues that apply only to new parents such as how long to let the baby cry before checking on her, what and how to discipline, and so forth. However, there is one issue over which new parents argue with each other more than any other. And the winner is (drumroll) . . . the division of the workload in the family. Yes, new parents fight more about who does what around the house than any other issue. In fact one study indicated that unrealized expectations over shared responsibilities accounts for a 10 percent overall decline in a husband's marital quality and a 25 percent overall decline in a wife's marital quality (i.e., her overall satisfaction with the marital relationship). The reason for this difference will be clearer in a minute.

Obviously, childless couples argue some about this as well. However, it's a whole new ballgame once baby comes into the picture. You may feel as though you had all of this worked out before you became new parents. In fact, you may be in that group of couples who felt that each of you did his or her fair share of running the household and that it was, for the most part, fairly equitable. Let me warn you that once a baby arrives, the deck gets reshuffled. Prepare to deal with this.

What Actually Happens?

This issue of dividing the workload has been studied pretty extensively among new parent couples. Based on this research, we can predict that for most couples the mother will end up carrying the overwhelming responsibility for managing the household and caring for their children during the first few years of parenting. In fact, mothers end up taking on even more than they expected before giving birth. This is true whether the mother works outside of the home or not. In one study, when the baby was six months old, both the mother and the father reported that mom was doing more and dad was doing less than *either* parent predicted before the baby was born. It seems that even among more "progressive" couples who agree that things should be divided equally, once the baby comes home, mom ends up shouldering most of the household and caring-for-the-baby tasks. Dad doesn't just sit back and watch more baseball or play more golf, however. It seems that most men actually increase their hours of paid, outside-the-home work once they become fathers. Thus, the default mode for most new parents appears to be that mom stays home initially and takes over the lioness's share of the home and baby chores while dad logs in more hours at work. Unfortunately, this usually doesn't lead to marital bliss.

A Downward Spiral

Let me tell you about a bad pattern that many new parents fall into with each other. Once mom and dad bring their new bundle home, mom begins to take over for the most part. She is consumed with feeding, changing, and monitoring the baby, along with other things, as she becomes comfortable in her new, exciting, and somewhat anxiety-producing role. While more and more women are returning to the workplace after taking some time off, most new mothers do take off from work for a while initially after giving birth. Consequently, they often pour themselves into the role of mother enthusiastically. As mom steps into this role, dad often steps back a bit. Granted, there are some new dads who are eager to jump in and take on their share of the tasks. However, it usually falls to mom, especially if she chooses to breastfeed.

Most men do not take much, if any, time off from work after the baby is born. While there are exceptions, it simply is true that the vast majority of mothers take an extended maternity leave postpartum while dads get back to work relatively quickly. I'll leave it to the activists to debate whether this is right or wrong, fair or unfair. It simply is the way it is. For many dads, there is a feeling of pressure to get back and bring in the income. This is particularly true if the couple is accustomed to budgeting based on both husband and wife working and her job has limited financial maternity leave benefits. Furthermore, work is an area where dad feels he can really contribute to the family. Mom may be able to breastfeed, but dad can bring home the bacon. In fact, for many dads I've talked with, they are rather proud of their selfless, long hours of work, which go to support the now expanded family.

On the home front we find mom, who is adjusting to a radical change in her life. If she worked outside the home prior to delivery, there is an even more drastic change in her life. She's traded business suits for warm-up suits. Conference calls have been replaced by diaper changes. Analyzing complicated spreadsheets and sales forecasts have been left behind for the thrill of cleaning up vomit. If mom did not work outside the home, the transition is still intense. As we talked about earlier, the feeling of unrelenting responsibility is overwhelming. Sleep patterns have been disrupted, and time spent with friends or in volunteer or leisure activities has diminished or disappeared altogether. Even women who know intellectually that things will be different are not prepared for the reality of the changes that occur. As we've said, she has taken over the majority of the household and baby chores.

In walks dad at the end of a long day at work, feeling like the good provider, only to find mom feeling "dumped on"—or worse, "abandoned"—by dad, who's been gone all day while she's "taken care of everything." In some cases, mom sees dad walking through the door at the end of the workday as a chance to finally catch a break. She's been at it all day long—taking care of a clingy, crying, needy baby. She has been busy all day and seems to have little to show for her endless, tireless effort at home. She is sleep-deprived, tired, and she feels unappreciated. It's been all she can do to keep up with the demands of her baby and to keep the house from being taken over by piles of toys and laundry. She envisions dad walking through the door, dropping his briefcase, and asking, "Hi, Honey. What can I do to help and where would you like to go for dinner?" *At last*, she thinks to herself, *I can relax for a few minutes.*

Dad, on the other hand, has been dealing with the usual stress of his job, is worried more than ever about making his quota and getting the bonus he budgeted for now that there's an extra mouth to feed, and has just fought through rush-hour traffic in a car that he now is wondering how long he'll keep before they have to upgrade to a minivan (i.e., more money). He envisions himself walking through the door to a home that is neat and tranquil, perhaps savoring the aroma of a home-cooked meal simmering on the stove (*After all, she's been home all day*, he figures), changing out of his work clothes, and relaxing on the couch until dinner is on the table. *At last*, he thinks, *I can relax for a few minutes*. The next scene is predictable:

Allen: Hi, Honey. I'm beat. What's for dinner?

Susan: Are you kidding me? I haven't even thought about dinner. Can you take Thomas for a few minutes? He's been fussy all day and I'm exhausted.

Allen: C'mon, I just got home. I'm starving. I need some downtime.

Susan: Yeah, well join the club!

Studies show the downward spiral that takes place as follows:

1. Mom takes on the majority of household and parenting tasks.
2. Dad gets more involved in work outside the home.
3. Mom becomes disappointed and resentful because of the lack of physical and emotional support she receives from dad.
4. Dad gets even more involved in work because he wants to avoid being criticized or unappreciated.

5. Mom becomes more and more isolated from social activities as demands at home increase, and she is too tired to do much beyond this.

6. Both mom and dad feel unappreciated and less connected, and their positive and affectionate interactions with each other decrease.

7. As time goes on . . . erosion of intimacy and closeness continues.

Ron and Patty

Ron and Patty are typical of many couples I see. Ron is a successful professional, and Patty is a stay-at-home mother. They are young, active, and energetic. They planned to have a family and were delighted from the moment they learned Patty was pregnant with Lauren. They would both describe their marriage as "better than most" prior to becoming parents. In fact, they still voice their love for and commitment to one another. However, they've recently hit a "snag" in their relationship. The following is an excerpt from a session with me:

> Patty: I can't handle how you always come home in a bad mood. I work hard all day and the last thing I need is to have you walk through the door ready to bite someone's head off.

> Ron: Look, you don't get it. I get up at 5:00 a.m. and start handling things the minute I walk through the door of the office. It's just one problem after another with the phones ringing and people demanding that I make time for them. Then I have to fight this ridiculous traffic to walk into a house with nothing

to eat and stuff scattered everywhere. What exactly do you do all day long?

Patty: What do you think I do all day? Who do you think takes care of Lauren? You have no idea what it's like to stay at home and watch after her. You must think I sit and watch TV eating bonbons all day long. I'd like to see you stay home one day and do what I do. You couldn't do it for one hour. [*Personal note: Why do people still refer to bonbons to make a point? I haven't seen a bonbon in decades.*]

The underlying theme to this argument is the feeling from both Ron and Patty that things are not fair. Ron confided to me privately that he feels that Patty has a "better deal" than he does. In his perspective, Patty gets to nap when the baby does, has little real "stress" from taking care of Lauren, has a much more flexible schedule, even gets to have leisurely lunches with the other moms in the neighborhood, and fails to appreciate how much he does for the family. Patty shares a much different view of the world. She feels that she never gets a "break" from being a parent. Ron gets to go off to work where he is admired and respected by other adults, have adult conversations about interesting things, and doesn't have a helpless baby tugging on him 24/7. It seems that for each of them, the grass is definitely greener on the other side of the fence.

It's Not Fair!

Research indicates that for new parents, each parent claims to be doing more than the other gives him or her credit for. In other words, almost all new parents feel that their spouses do not acknowledge or appreciate everything that they are doing.

There is usually a feeling that *I'm doing more and you don't see it*. The data tells us that it is this *perception of unfairness* that gets couples into trouble. In fact, the actual amount of time spent on tasks seems to be much less important than whether or not each person *felt* that the final division of labor was fair or unfair.

There also seems to be a subtle difference between men and women regarding this issue. For men, it appears that the process of how things are divided up is very important. This may be consistent with the way men do things. Most men don't really like to be told what to do. They like to feel like they have a say in the matter. It seems that men do much better when the list of what has to get done is discussed and reasoned out before chores are assigned or agreed upon. If men feel that there has been a discussion about dividing things up and that their input has been considered, they may feel more like it is a fair process and may be more likely to participate with a good attitude. Perhaps this is the reason men talk so disdainfully about their "honey-do" lists—men just don't like to be assigned chores; they like to take part in the discussion on the front end.

For women, it seems that what matters most is whether or not their husbands are seen as getting involved in taking care of the baby and helping out around the house. This last point is huge. In fact, if a woman feels that her husband is making a fair contribution to baby and house chores, there is some evidence that she will experience an *increase* in satisfaction with the marital relationship. Yes, some moms who feel that dads are pitching in actually feel *more* satisfied with their marriages than before. This cuts both ways, however. When a mom feels that dad is not helping out or is not involved enough, there is a significant decrease in her satisfaction with the marriage.

Suggestions for Resolving Conflict over Chores

There's no doubt about it: once you have a baby, you will have to shuffle the chore cards around. What worked before almost certainly will no longer be effective. This is the biggest area of conflict among new parents, and it has serious ramifications for the couple's relationship as it accounts for a significant portion of decline in marital satisfaction, particularly for wives. It makes sense to work it out. Let me offer a few suggestions on how you might approach this very important topic:

1. Talk about who did what before.

Most couples just fall into a routine of getting things done. Few sit down, make a list of chores, and assign each to one or both of them. For couples who fight about this, one or both of them feels that there is an unfair distribution of labor. This is a sign that things need to be discussed. You probably needed to do this anyway. If neither of you felt there was inequity in who did what, you probably fell into a pattern of getting things done that worked well for you. Unfortunately, this does not mean that it will automatically feel this way after adding a baby to your family. If you are still expecting your first child, you can start by listing who does what household tasks currently. If you are in the postdelivery phase, start by listing who does what and then list what doesn't get done at all but needs to get done.

2. Acknowledge that things need to be redistributed.

Remember that bringing a new baby into the home changes everything. Don't be naïve enough to think that "things will just work out." Remember that the research shows us that if you are not proactive about this, mom will get stuck with most of the chores and will end up becoming resentful that dad isn't helping. This is what is referred to in the professional world as a "lose-lose" solution in a relationship, and it will start you down a bad marital path. Don't go there! This area is a big one. No one relishes the idea of sitting down to talk about chores. How boring! Furthermore, who wants to have a discussion that might result in you having to do more work? The truth is, there are many reasons to talk yourself out of sitting down and discussing this area of responsibility. However, as unappealing as chore chat may be, it will save you tons of grief down the road.

3. Write down all the things that you think need to be done in a week or a month.

Allow the list to be flexible—you'll probably have to add some things to it that you forgot initially. It is very important that both of you come up with the list. If one makes the list and hands it to the other, you are off to a bad start. This is a list that is made *together*. This can be accomplished by making one list at the same time or by making two separate lists (one made by each of you) which is merged into a single one at a later time. The point is that there must be a joint contribution to the process. It may be helpful to just keep a running list of things that get done or need to be done for two weeks. Each time someone does a task, he or she lists it and put his or her name beside it. If there is an obvious task that no one is doing (for example, you both continue to step over a pile of laundry sitting there for two weeks), put it on the list and place a question mark beside the task—it will get taken care of in the next step.

***4. The fun begins! Start assigning each task on the list to each
person or to both of you together.***

Everything on the list is now up for grabs. Each task can be
reassigned if necessary. On a separate sheet of paper (or dry erase
board, or whatever), begin by listing each chore and assigning
it to one of you. The process works best if each of you volunteer
to do all of the things you are already doing and are willing to
continue doing. Assign these tasks first by listing the task and
putting your name beside your chore. Some of the items will
undoubtedly be shared responsibilities, so they will have both
of your names beside them. With the remaining items, try to
divide them up as fairly as possible. This can be tricky. One
way to do this is to try to estimate together how much time
each task would require to complete. This gives you a starting
point. Obviously, three chores that would take two hours each
to complete cannot be compared to three chores that take
fifteen minutes each to complete. Fairness may be measured
in time. Then again, there may be some tasks that one of you
finds particularly difficult for various reasons. These should be
stated up front and traded out as needed. For example, my wife
and I worked out a deal regarding two of the more unpleasant
tasks associated with young babies. I have a strong aversion
to vomit. I think I was traumatized as a child by vomit (true
story): I recall sitting in Sunday school and seeing a young girl
suddenly projectile vomit across the room in my direction. I
still get a bit queasy when I think about it. I told Dana when
the boys were young, "Honey, I'll clean up any type of mess
the kids can make, but I can't do vomit."

One Christmas Eve, we went to get our youngest son out of
his crib to join us for Christmas dinner. He had been unusually
quiet, which is almost always a bad sign. Somehow, his diaper

had come loose, and he discovered that poop can be used as an art supply. As my wife and I stood frozen and horrified at the entrance to his room, our oldest son (still a toddler at the time) walked in, saw (and smelled) his young brother engaged in his art project, and immediately vomited on the floor directly in front of the crib. There was no discussion regarding who would clean up what. We both understood that the vomit was hers and the poop was mine. It's been a fair trade-off ever since.

Fairness is one of those concepts that everyone understands in theory, but has trouble working out in reality. The biggest reason for this is that most of us have a lot of trouble seeing things from another person's perspective as clearly as we see it from our own. It's like I tell my two boys, "If you constantly try to see the fairness in every interaction, both of you will ultimately believe that you are getting the short end of the stick." Human nature dictates that when something is unfair in our favor we naturally overlook it, but when something is unfair in someone else's favor it gets our full attention. Don't expect the chore list to feel completely fair and balanced. The point is to work together with some empathy for each other's roles so that things feel *approximately fair*.

5. Stay on the same team as you work it out.

It is important to approach this process with the mindset of "It's us against the *to-do* list." This has to feel like a win-win game. I've played sports most of my life, and as an adult, I consult for a professional sports team. I have never seen a team at any level function effectively when the team members turn against one another. In order for your home to function effectively, you and your spouse must be on the same team and you must work together to accomplish your goals. Your job is to work *as a team* to make sure that what has to get done gets done without either of you feeling exploited, bullied, manipulated, or taken advantage of. If you find yourself getting into adversarial positions, take a break until you can come back at it together. Keep saying to one another, "We're on the same team—let's work together."

6. Experiment and revisit.

Sometimes it is important to try things out for a while. In other words, if you are having trouble agreeing on who does some of the things that need to get done, come up with a solution and try it for two weeks. Agree that at the end of two weeks you will sit down to discuss whether or not it is working. I find that people frequently resist agreeing to some solution because they feel that once they do, they are bound by that agreement forever. It is as though once they agree that they will clean the bathroom, it is as binding as a Supreme Court decision, complete with no option to appeal.

> Fred: I know I agreed to clean the bathrooms, but I'm getting tired of it, and it's really too much for me to do right now with this project at work hanging over my head.

> Elaine: What? But you agreed to it. You clearly agreed that you would clean the bathrooms. You can't back out now.

> Fred: Yeah, but . . .

> Elaine: But nothing! Are you a man of your word or not? You said you would do it. You promised! How can I ever believe you if you don't keep your commit-

ments? You said you would do it! Where do you
think you're going?

Fred: [*Walking away with his head hung down*] To find the
Lysol.

Good luck getting Fred to agree on anything in the future.
When agreements on household chores are treated as requiring the same commitment as a thirty-year fixed-rate mortgage,
people are reticent to sign on the dotted line. Allowing agreements regarding household chores to be "experiments" that can be
tried for a brief time and then reevaluated results in an increased
willingness to try them out. Make agreements time-limited and
give each other the option of saying, "That didn't work for me;
let's keep trying to find a solution." Oftentimes, I have found
couples saying that they were sure that they had agreed to take
on too much and that it would feel unfair, only to find that at the
end of two weeks, it did not feel that way at all. Of course, if it
does, renegotiate and try for another two weeks. Before you know
it, your situation at home will change as your child or children
grow older, and your household chore distribution list will need
to be modified anyway.

7. Dads, remember how important it is to get involved in these tasks.

The data are very clear on this one. The couples who do the best
report that dads have rolled up their sleeves and have jumped in
to pitch in. Some of you dads are rolling your eyes and thinking,
Great, how fair is that? Just trust me on this one. You've heard the
old adage "If momma ain't happy, ain't nobody happy" or "Happy
wife—happy life"? You will ultimately benefit by heeding my

advice. Besides, I'm going to advocate for you in another chapter, so hang with me. Dad's involvement is especially important for couples who have decided for Mom to stay home full-time. The point here is to avoid the mentality of "I have a full-time job. If she's going to stay home with the baby, why should I have to do that stuff?" There's no reason both of you should not feel a sense of shared responsibility. Sure, if you work and your wife is staying home with the baby, it makes sense that for the majority of the day she is taking care of household and baby tasks while you are at the office or job worksite. However, once you get home, why should you feel that you are "done" while she continues to do her job until bedtime? That doesn't exactly sound fair to me (and I'm a man!). If both of you work outside the home, then it is pretty clear that you should be willing to pitch in with after-work household and baby chores.

There is another benefit for dad when he is willing to get involved in these tasks at home. I have found that this can be a wonderful opportunity for dad to begin to bond with his new baby. It is easy for dads to feel somewhat on the perimeter of what is taking place between mother and baby in the early months. I strongly suggest that dads take over bathing and getting baby ready for bed in the evening. Talk about a win-win strategy: mom gets a much-needed break in the evening and dad gets to spend special one-on-one time with baby. I did this for our boys, and I highly recommend it.

8. Keep your perspective—this situation is temporary.

The redistribution of tasks that you agree to is not for the remainder of your lives. Having a new baby in your house is a series of stages that change rapidly. Your baby won't always be so helpless and need such constant attention. Neither of you will be so exhausted forever. The first year is difficult for many reasons—everything is new, your baby is at his or her neediest, simple errands require much more planning and preparation, and so on. Dads may have to pick up more of the slack in the first year or two while mom is more overwhelmed by the demands of a new baby, and then it evens out. However, keep your perspective. Remember, at this stage of the game "the days are long, but the years are short."

9. Let some things go.

This should go without saying, but for some of you I need to say it anyway. When you bring a baby home, don't be afraid to let a few things go. Again, this is a temporary stage. It is perfectly okay to eat take-out more often than before, vacuum less often, and not force yourself to do everything as you did it before. Your new baby demands a great deal of time, and you are probably more sleep-deprived and exhausted than you have been since your freshman year in college (without all the fun). Therefore, if there were some tasks that you both did before that can be put on a shelf for a little while—do it!

10. Learn the beauty of "good enough."

This goes along with number 9. People vary greatly regarding where they fall on the continuum of perfectionism. For perfectionists, making the transition to parent is particularly difficult. Getting everything done that needs getting done may mean lowering your standards in some areas or completely letting things go in other areas. What used to be a clean house now needs to be a clean-enough house. A good dinner may need to be an adequate one. An unmade bed here and there or a little clutter never hurt anyone. (Not too much clutter, however, because this contributes to a chaotic environment, which leads to other problems as we discussed earlier.) When your child gets a little older and you have a little more time, you can go back to your usual standards of perfection. (Actually, when your child becomes a teenager, you will have to learn this lesson all over again, but that's another book entirely.) Allow your standard of perfection to drop down to "good enough" for a while. You may be surprised at what a difference this will make. Additionally, you will probably learn that the things you thought "had to be done" don't really make that much of a difference in your quality of life after all.

Household chores are inescapable. Bringing children into the home only increases chores and makes your former system obsolete. Rick Carlson in *Don't Sweat the Small Stuff with Your Family* suggests that families view household chores like painting the Golden Gate Bridge in San Francisco. Apparently, a crew of full-time painters works year-round to maintain the bridge's paint job. However, their job is never really "finished." It's an ongoing process. Household chores are the same—there's always something to do. Arguing over how household chores are divided up after a baby comes home is the biggest source of conflict for most couples. Make a decision to approach this area of your life as a team, and don't let it result in strife, resentment, and dissatisfaction in your relationship.

5

Some Advice for Moms

I am writing this chapter specifically to mothers-to-be or to new moms. It's okay for fathers-to-be or new dads to read it as well (in fact, I encourage it). However, I will use the pronoun *you* to speak directly to moms. According to Dr. Gottman's research in the area of couples becoming new parents, there is one thing that dramatically reduces the risk of marital satisfaction declining once baby comes and makes the family three. It is simply this: if fathers follow mothers into the role of parenting rather than watching from the sidelines, the outcome for the marriage is much better. This may seem obvious, but it is not necessarily common. There are some reasons why you and your husband transform into parents very differently. Understanding these differences may help you facilitate the transformation more effectively for yourself and for your husband.

For new mothers (you), the transition to motherhood is usually natural and dramatic. The mother-baby bond is often primitive, instinctual, and overwhelming. The shift that occurs in your priorities is nothing short of a complete metamorphosis. However, the change is not the same for men. In fact, for most men, the "bonding" that takes place with a new child often occurs later and more gradually than it does for mothers. It is not less meaningful or intense once it occurs, but it happens differently for most men than for women. This doesn't mean that dad loves the newborn less than you—it just takes more time for him to make the shift from husband to father than it does for you to make the shift from wife to mother. It may be helpful to understand that there are some hormonal changes that you go through during pregnancy and lactation that actually predispose and prepare you to be more parental than your husband. It's as though your brain is sending the right programming to prepare you for the dramatic shift that is occurring. Unfortunately, the male brain undergoes no such reprogramming. This is a fundamental biological difference in the sexes as it relates to the change from spouse to parent.

An interesting study done by Carolyn Pape Cowan and Philip Cowan illustrated how this change in roles occurs. The Cowans found that the part of "self" that you identify as "mother" increases from around 10 percent to 34 percent from late pregnancy to after you deliver your baby and remains there for several years. Picture a big circle that represents "you." Now when women are asked to indicate how much of that entire circle represents the part of them that they identify as "mother," that portion increased from about 10 percent of the entire circle to 34 percent of the circle. By contrast, the part of "self" that husbands labeled "father" during their wives' pregnancies is about half that of women labeling themselves as "mother" during the same time. By the time a child is eighteen months old, a husband's identity as "parent" is about one-third as large as that of his wife's (Cowan & Cowan, 2000).

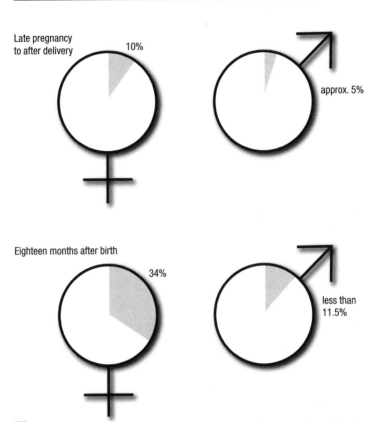

Part of "self" that women identify as "mother" or part of "self" men identify as "father." Entire circle represents the whole person.

In other words, in the early stages of parenting, the role of "mother" becomes much larger for you than the role of "father" becomes for your husband. Once again, this does not suggest that you love your new baby more than your husband, but rather that the role of parent simply feels more consuming to you than to him.

What's It Like for New Fathers?

I've spoken with lots of new dads, and I've been one myself. It might be helpful if you gain a little understanding into what it's really like for many new dads. To be fair, you've got your hands full with the new tasks of motherhood and the process of transitioning into the most important role of your life. Yet, for the sake of your marriage, I would ask you to remember that your husband's experience of becoming a father is going to be very different than yours of becoming a mother. We men are notorious for not letting on when we feel intimidated, confused, or hurt. The old joke about men not asking for directions is based on a good deal of truth about the male psyche. It is unlikely that your husband will let you know some of the struggles that most men have with the transition to fatherhood. My purpose for writing a separate chapter for you and your husband is to help each of you see what the other's experience may be like a little more clearly. If I can help you gain a better understanding of what your husband may be going through, the transition into parenthood for both of you will feel much more like a shared experience.

What about Me?

The bond you feel with your new baby is or will be an experience unlike any other you've known. Clearly, there are some exceptions—such as women who experience postpartum depression. However, most of you will immediately experience a connection with your newborn that is palpable. In fact, for most of you, this has been happening during your pregnancy. Guys get to witness the miracle of a new life growing inside of you. However, this is nothing compared to actually carrying a new life around for nine months. Consider the difference between watching someone ski down a black diamond slope and actually doing it yourself! You have bonded with your new baby during your pregnancy while we dads have to be content as spectators. It just isn't the same experience.

Then, once the magical day finally arrives, you get to hold that newborn and finally meet the one you've been sustaining for these long nine months. There's really no other relationship to which you can compare this feeling. While most of us dads can appreciate the connection, we typically just don't react the same way initially. In fact, there's often a little feeling of jealousy that men may suppress. Freud came up with the Oedipus complex which described the jealousy that a young boy may feel toward his father because of dad's "special" relationship with his mother. (By the way, most psychologists don't put much faith in Freud's theories anymore.) However, I'm convinced that more common is an initial difficulty new fathers have with the "special" relationship that newborns have with their wives. It's difficult for most new dads not to feel that they are just a little excluded from this relationship. (I'm not familiar enough with Greek mythology to come up with a cool sounding name for this "complex.")

This is sometimes exacerbated by your understandable fascination and preoccupation with your new baby. Let's face it—you are watching every coo and gas pain with the greatest of intensity. The truth is, you didn't pay this much attention to your husband even when you were dating (although his gas pains may have caught your attention). Chances are that by the time baby arrives, you aren't going to be very tuned in to your husband at all. If you choose to breastfeed your newborn, you are on call around the clock. Breastfeeding is an especially bonding experience from which most dads feel excluded. I recall watching that special bonding take place as my wife breastfed both of our boys. It was great to see this wonderful and natural process of mother-infant love, but I was not much of an integral part of the process.

Not all new mothers immediately transition joyfully into motherhood. Research (Feeney, Hohaus, Noller, & Alexander, 2001; Lyles, 2002) shows that about 58 percent of new mothers will experience something called "baby blues" or postpartum blues. This is a term that describes *mild* sadness, irritability, and moodiness that occurs within the first two weeks following delivery and may continue for hours or days. Most of the time it is mild and gets better on its own. However, between 5 and 20 percent of women experience something more severe known as postpartum depression (PPD). This is a condition that resembles full-blown clinical depression in new mothers and may require medical attention. If you find yourself feeling seriously depressed (e.g., feelings of hopelessness, unable to get motivated to do anything, serious sleep and appetite changes, difficulty experiencing any happiness, possible suicidal thoughts or feelings), you should talk with your doctor. PPD is more serious than the "baby blues" and may not just go away after a few days. However, there are treatments that help if you talk with your doctor.

Another factor that may exacerbate the feeling of being on the outside for dads is the reaction that a newborn may give dad. Because you are often more involved in the early stages of infant care, your new baby is becoming familiar with you. There is a feeling of comfort and safety that is associated with you. He may smile and light up when he sees your face. This association may not be as strong with dad. In fact, at times, dad can pick up a content new baby from mom's arms only to be greeted by a bloodcurdling scream. This is often followed by mom quickly taking the baby back and settling him down in a matter of seconds. The result is dad feeling like a total stranger—and an unwelcome one, at that.

"You're Not Really Going to Do It like That Are You?"

As if it's not bad enough that we feel like we've been left at the station as the mom-and-baby train speed toward happily-ever-after without us, when we do try to act like a parent, you can sometimes make us feel like complete incompetent idiots. I know that you don't really mean to make us feel this way—it's just that when we find that we are changing the diaper wrong, holding the baby wrong, burping the baby wrong, have placed him in the crib wrong, are feeding him wrong, and on and on, we begin to feel like we're just in the way. And that's not the worst of it. There are times when you also make us feel like we're actually harboring some secret desire to commit infanticide. This is communicated by emphatic statements such as, "What is wrong with you? Don't you know he could choke on that and die? I can't even leave you alone with him for a second!" It's bad enough to feel incompetent—but being accused of attempted homicide is a bit more than our already fragile egos can handle.

Where'd You Go?

Many new fathers start to feel not like they have gained a new member of the family but that they've lost their wives. You just aren't there anymore. Again, I am not suggesting that any of this is deliberate. However, the experience many new fathers share is that they become either invisible, or worse—an obstacle in their own home. New dads feel that you are so preoccupied with caring for your new baby that *they* could come home wearing a new dress with high heels and you'd barely notice. All the little things you used to do to show you care are now things you are doing for the new baby. And don't even get me started on sex. I realize that in the early months (maybe years?) of child rearing, sex is often the farthest thing from your mind, but not from your husband's! According to some research conducted by Shaunti Feldhahn (2004), men secretly believe that your love for them is revealed by how much you want to have sex with them. If you show little to no interest in having sex with your husband, he will frequently interpret this as meaning that you really don't love him anymore. The old stereotype that men are only interested in the physical aspect of sex appears to be an incorrect one after all!

It All Adds Up To . . .

When you combine the fact that you and your new baby have this magical bond that dad is watching from the bleachers, that new dads are getting the message that they are incompetent or even dangerous, and that they've lost their wives to motherhood, the outcome is often deleterious to a marriage. The tragic response of most men to feeling unwanted and incompetent is to withdraw. Yep, we just shut down. You already know that the male ego is a fragile thing. We don't handle rejection or failure very well at all. However, unlike you, we don't typically cry and talk about it—we just say, "Forget it!" There's some biological thing in most men that causes them to get angry and check out when they feel they are unwanted and unappreciated. It's true—ask any man. Why do you think a professional athlete at the top of his game asks to be traded as soon as he feels he is not appreciated by his team or the fans? It's not for the money! When a new dad starts to feel unwanted and unappreciated by you, he begins to withdraw. This is the beginning of trouble for your marriage. In order for your marriage to survive this critical shift, I have some specific advice for you—the mom-to-be or new mom:

Understand His Experience

I believe that much of what I just shared has come as a surprise to many of you. You are so enamored and thrilled with your new role, you couldn't imagine your husband not sharing this experience with you. However, if you can understand what it is like for your husband during this time, it will undoubtedly help ease the transition into parenthood for both of you.

My wife tells me that there is no way a man can begin to understand what the experience of being pregnant and giving birth is like. I'm sure she's right. I believe that it is important that both husbands and wives realize that it is impossible to really know what it is like to be the other. Therefore, it is imperative that you put a great deal of effort into trying your best to see life through your husband's eyes as much as possible. The best scenario for a couple with a new baby is for them to go through the transition, feeling that they are experiencing parenthood as a team. Far too many fathers tell me that they feel like they are a backup singer rather than singing a duet with their wife. If your husband feels that you understand what the transition may be like on his end, he is more likely to feel that he is part of the process with you.

Encourage His Involvement

This may be the most difficult but most important recommendation I can offer you: encourage and allow your husband to be a dad, *even if he doesn't do it the way you think he should!* I cannot emphasize this point enough. In order for your husband to follow you into parenthood, he needs to feel like an integral part of the team. Being part of the team makes it easier for dad to develop an all-important bond with his child.

During the first year of parenthood for me and my wife, Dana took her role as mom very seriously and was good at it. I was thrilled to be a new dad, and I loved Caleb very much. However, I must admit, the bonding switch had not flipped for me in the same way it had for Dana during the first few months. We had moved into a new house, and our hardwood floors needed to be refinished, requiring us to stay in a hotel for a couple of nights. So we checked in one Saturday to stay for the weekend.

Dana had not had a real opportunity to go out on her own for a while, so I stayed with Caleb for most of the day while she went to the hair salon, ran a few errands, and took care of other things she'd been itching to get done. She was gone only for a few hours. When she came back that evening, she walked in and within a few minutes commented, "What happened today? Something's different." She was right. I can't explain what happened that afternoon, but during the course of being one-on-one with Caleb, something very real and important took place—it was as though someone flipped a switch and a connection was made between us that has been present ever since that day over twelve years ago.

I had the same experience with our second son, Ben: as I got involved in caring for him, the bond formed strongly and persists to this day. I am convinced that it is completely necessary for dads to be involved in the hands-on care of new babies during the first few years in order to maximize this bond between father and child. There is some research that supports the fact that fathers who participate in the day-to-day care of young children report stronger and more satisfying relationships with them as they grow older.

In order for this to happen, you must encourage and allow it to. Don't insist, nag, or demand—this approach results in a whole

other set of relationship dynamics. Besides, I highlight the importance of dad getting involved in my chapter to dads. However, you
can encourage and allow your husband's involvement by refusing
to criticize the way he does things. In fact, don't even instruct
him unless he asks. Contrary to some old stereotypes, most of us
are not the bumbling idiots we're portrayed as being. We actually
do have a little common sense. And by all means, *never* suggest
that we would put our own children at risk—this is insulting
and very hurtful. (Note: Obviously, I am addressing the normal
differences in the way moms and dads parent. Unfortunately, I
have witnessed isolated incidents of a parent who is abusive or
neglectful to a child. While beyond the scope of this book, if you
feel that your husband is abusive or neglectful, you need to seek
professional help immediately.)

The research is very clear that moms and dads have a different
approach to parenting and very different styles. Guess what? There
are distinct *advantages* to both ways—one is not superior to the
other. For example, dads tend to be more physical and rough-
and-tumble in play than moms, who adapt a more caretaking
style and follow the child's initiatives more often. The way dad
plays with a child tends to nurture and emphasize characteristics
such as challenge, competition, initiative, independence, and
risk-taking while mom's play tends to emphasize caretaking,
safety, and emotional security. All of these characteristics are
healthy and important and should be valued. When it comes
to discipline, dads tend to emphasize rules and limits and to be
firmer and more matter-of-fact whereas moms tend to be more
responsive to the child's temperament and the situation and to
explain and negotiate. Again, it is the balance of these styles that
results in optimal outcomes for children.

For you moms who get nervous with dad's style of interaction, you should know that research is very clear regarding the benefits of dad's early involvement in your child's life. Children whose fathers are actively involved in their children's lives exhibit higher verbal and math skills along with better problem solving and overall school achievement than children whose fathers are less involved. Accept the different way he changes the diaper, bathes the baby, feeds the baby, and so forth. Remind yourself that every time he is involved in caring for the baby, a bond is forming, and your child—as well as your marriage—is likely to benefit.

One thing you may have to watch out for is a subtle feeling of being threatened by dad's involvement. This is particularly true for stay-at-home moms who feel threatened if dad becomes too active or very skilled at taking care of the baby. Some subtle insecurities can arise causing you to unconsciously sabotage dad's efforts. Some moms have stated that they have had to deal with feelings such as, *If he can take care of the baby as well as I can, what's my purpose?* Don't worry, you are irreplaceable. The more dad is involved and the better he is at it, the better for everyone.

Make Him Feel Part of the Process

If you are a stay-at-home mom, it is especially easy for your husband to feel left out. You are there to witness so much of what is happening. Of course I realize that it's not a day full of gazing in wonderment at your new baby. There is little glamour in parenting in the early years. However, there are things that happen during the day that dad misses. It helps to include him by sharing some of the more memorable moments with him. Unless it is a real interruption during the day, it can be nice to make a phone call to check in with him. Today's technology also makes it a little easier to stay connected during a busy day (e.g., text message a short "I love you," send a cute snapshot of you and baby with a phone camera, or just send a quick email letting him know you and baby are thinking about him). At the end of the day, it is nice to share anything special that happened as your baby grows and develops. This really varies from couple to couple; however, for some dads, this helps them feel part of the process.

He Still Thinks He Is a Husband as well as a Father

As we stated earlier, the transition from wife to mother is often more dramatic than the transition from husband to father. Therefore, it is not uncommon for a new mother to fall completely into her role as mom and really have fewer "wife" needs. Your husband, on the other hand, has plenty of his "husband" needs left. Remember, his transition occurs differently. Research tends to support the differences between new moms and new dads in this area as well (Cowan & Cowan, 2000). When you are pregnant, the part of your "self" that you label as "partner" or "lover" is exactly the same as your husband. However, at six months after your baby arrives, your part of "self" you label as "partner" or "lover" has shrunk to 22 percent while your husband's part of "self" labeled as "partner" or "lover" has decreased only to 30 percent. If you looked at this on a pie chart, you would see that your husband's needs in this area cover just less than one-third of his pie, while yours is just over one-fifth of the whole pie.

In other words, your "mother" part has squeezed your "lover" part out of the picture some—much more so than for your husband. His "lover" part did not get taken over by his "father" part as much.

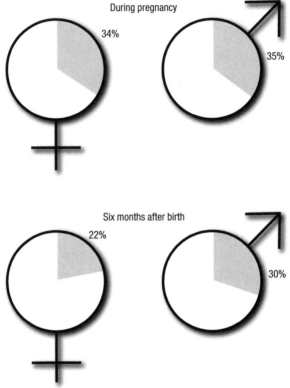

Wife   **Husband**

During pregnancy

34%

35%

Six months after birth

22%

30%

Part of "self" that a person identifies as "partner" or "lover"

It is almost like the old television show *Batman*: Bruce Wayne would slide down the pole into the Bat Cave and by the time he got to the bottom of the pole, Wayne had transformed completely into Batman. When you slid down the motherhood pole, you landed as a fully transformed mom—cape and all. However, your husband landed in the Parenthood Cave still looking and feeling like Bruce Wayne. He still feels like a husband—complete with the needs of a husband. For the most part, these needs are for respect, affection, and appreciation. These three things are like water and sunlight to a plant. Unfortunately, most new moms give most, if not all, of their affection and appreciation to the new baby. I would encourage you to save some of these for your husband. Nothing minimizes the feeling of being left out like being told and shown that you are appreciated. Men rarely voice that this is important to them, but it is vital to them. In addition, most men need their wives' affection. This can be in the form of hugs, hand-holding, cuddling on the couch, or simply a smile.

Sometimes it is helpful to just let your husband know that you haven't forgotten about him. Letting him know that your decreased interest in and attention to him is not because he is less attractive or appealing to you is incredibly important. Remember, a man's ego is quite delicate. Just saying something like "I know it must feel like I'm not as attentive or interested in you lately. I hope you understand that it's not because I love you less or find you less appealing, I'm just consumed by my new role. I know it's a temporary thing, and I hope you will understand" can really be very affirming, validating, and reassuring to your husband.

So mom, your marital relationship is more likely to continue to grow in a positive direction as you and your husband transform into parents together. It is a more natural transition for you than for your husband. I hope that this chapter helps you understand how it occurs differently for each of you, and that these suggestions will help you facilitate this transformation with your husband.

6

For Dads

Man to Man

This chapter is written specifically for dads-to-be or new dads. Obviously your wives will read it as well since wives read everything related to areas they are interested in. We men only read the part of the directions we believe to be absolutely essential. This is the only chapter of the book where the pronoun *you* refers specifically to dad. Some of what I will say in this chapter is redundant to what I have written in the chapter to moms. However, I wanted to tell you how I think it applies to you and what you can do about it.

Just the Facts, Please

Since you are a guy, this will be a short chapter. If you're like most men, if it looks too wordy, you won't read it—I know; I'm the same way. I tried to come up with a way to make this chapter consist solely of illustrations, diagrams, and charts. Unfortunately, I could not come up with any good visuals to convey these concepts. Therefore, I'll give you the bottom line using the minimum of verbiage:

1. Your wife is going to turn, or has already turned, into a different person. Becoming pregnant results in some hormonal changes in her brain that turn her into a person who's very different from the woman you married. Before you get too frightened, it's probably a good thing that it happens this way. It will help her to become the kind of devoted mother that your baby needs.

2. The only problem is that you won't experience this same type of radical transformation in the same way she does. This could cause problems, but it doesn't have to.

3. The most important thing to know is that you can't stop your wife from changing into a mother. You can, however, change with her so that you don't feel so left behind. The bad news is that this is the only good choice you have. The good news is that if you choose wisely, your marriage will grow, and you will experience a new closeness with your wife as well as your new baby.

4. Finally, there is a group of men who have discovered the secret to making their wives and themselves happy, even through the stressful transition from couple to parents. I share this at the end of the chapter. (Most of you will now skip to the end and see what this secret is. Go ahead, I know I can't stop you; but you really should read the rest of this chapter as well—after all, it's not that long.)

Go with the Flow

When your wife became pregnant, a bond between her and your new baby began. For a woman, carrying a new life for nine months is an intense experience. It's neat for us dads as well, but it's just not the same as having a baby grow inside you for that long. There's really nothing we can compare this to—perhaps building a custom chopper from scratch comes to mind, but even that isn't close to having a baby grow inside you. Once the baby comes, the bond between mother and child is legendary. Don't worry if you don't feel the same bond as intensely as your wife does—that's natural in the first few months. However, try not to be threatened by your wife's preoccupation/obsession with the new baby. I know it can feel a little lonely, but it's normal and healthy. Just appreciate the fact that nature is taking its course.

Dealing with Your Feelings

I know that it's a risk to ask a guy to read what a psychologist has to say about feelings, but trust me—you need to read this section. It is common for new dads to struggle with feelings that no one warned you about. For example, you may find that you feel a little jealous that your new baby is getting all of your wife's attention and affection. Since no one really talks about this, most new dads just think that they must be feeling something wrong and stuff those feelings deep down where you put what it felt like to get picked on by the neighborhood bully when you were in kindergarten.

You may even start to resent the fact that you've been left out of this special relationship between your wife and your baby. Again, this is not unusual. You may also struggle with the fact that your wife isn't as available for you in many ways. This can cause feelings of disappointment, hurt, and even anger. If you don't recognize these kinds of feelings, you will probably "act out." That is psychobabble for expressing your negative feelings like anger by your indirect actions rather than directly.

For example, if you are mad at your wife about something and instead of going to her directly, you just "forget" to fix that leaky faucet she's been complaining about for a long time—that could be a form of "acting out" your anger. Acting out will usually get you in trouble and cause you more problems. That's why it's important to deal with feelings up front. "Dealing with feelings" is more psychobabble that just means recognizing how you feel, understanding it, accepting it, and deciding what you are going to do about it—even if that means simply waiting until the feelings change. The good news is that the feelings probably will change.

If You Can't Beat 'Em, Join 'Em . . .

The research on the difference in the ways men and women transition into parenthood is crystal clear: your marriage has the best chance of a good outcome after you become parents if *you* follow your wife down the road of parenthood wholeheartedly (Gottman & Silver, 2000). Yes, the burden once again falls on your shoulders. Moms make the transition involuntarily. For you, it'll require a little effort. Here are a few pointers:

Roll Up Your Sleeves

The best way to follow your wife down the parenting path is to get directly involved in the hands-on day-to-day care of your newborn. That means everything except breastfeeding. However, I'm told that they actually make a device (a strap-on breast—no, I'm not kidding!) that allows dad to simulate the act of breastfeeding. Okay, you don't have to go that far unless you really want to. (As Seinfeld might say, "Not that there's anything wrong with that.") However, it does mean changing diapers, bathing, bottle-feeding, burping, and all the rest. When our boys were infants and my wife would breastfeed, I was the DB—designated burper. After our boys would finish, I would see to it that they were properly and thoroughly purged of any excess tummy gas. It was awesome! Consider it a warm-up for the time they turn nine or ten years old and you get to teach them how to really belch one out like a man!

You "real men" may be imagining me as some kind of effeminate, touchy-feely psychologist who just thinks that guys should be like women. Since you don't know me, I should tell you that I've been accused of lots of things, but being a "girlie man" just isn't one of them. I can burp, scratch myself, and spit with the best of you, and I am the team psychologist for a professional basketball team. I like guy stuff, so don't think I'm trying to turn you into a woman. I'm trying to give you some solid advice to help the future of your marriage.

Some of you guys may be like the one who reacted to my advice to start getting more involved in the day-to-day care of his new baby by saying, "Are you kidding me? That's 'squaw' work." I certainly hope that this is not your attitude. If it is, I'd suggest you go ahead and put this book down and perhaps look for a good book on how to have an amicable divorce, because I can predict only bad things for your marriage in the future. Seriously, my advice for you to get involved is in everyone's best interest, especially your child's. Consider the following research findings:

- A study of more than 1,200 children showed that children whose fathers share meals, spend leisure time with them, or help them with reading or homework do significantly better academically than those children whose fathers do not (Cooksey & Fondell, 1996).
- A twenty-six-year longitudinal study on hundreds of individuals found that the single most important childhood fac-

119

tor in developing empathy is father involvement (Koestner, Franz, & Weinberger, 1990).

- Using a sample of almost one thousand households from the National Survey of Families and Households, researchers found that even after taking into account mothers' involvement, when fathers were highly involved in their children's lives, those children showed fewer behavioral problems (Amato & Rivera, 1999).

- One study showed that when adolescents rated their fathers high on nurturance, they were less likely to engage in deviant social behavior including drug use, truancy, and stealing (Barnes, 1984).

These are just a few of the studies demonstrating the benefits of a father's involvement in the life of a child. For more great information about the benefits of being an involved dad and to get some practical advice on the subject, I highly recommend becoming a member of the National Fatherhood Initiative (www.fatherhood.org). These guys are friends of mine and are great advocates of fatherhood.

Furthermore, the bond between you and your child will form and strengthen as you get involved in day-to-day care. I speak from experience on these matters. There is a ton of research on the importance of early infant-caretaker attachment on the developing personality and emotional well-being of your baby. Most of this is focused on mom. However, I firmly believe that this attachment with you in the first two years is vital for your child's future.

Go Back to School

Another way to get involved is to join your wife on her quest for information. By now, you've got all kinds of books on every topic related to babies and parenting. While you don't have to read them all (bonus points if you do), you can ask your wife what she's been picking up from these resources and learn what she's learning. Who knows, you actually might learn something. At the very least, you are joining with her in the process of becoming a more educated parent.

Don't Take It Personally

I know that some of you will object by saying that you would be happy to get involved if your wife would let you. I've written a chapter for her on this topic. But let's face it, no matter how hard she tries, she won't be able to bite her tongue forever. She will probably tell you that you are doing something wrong when you try to bathe, change, feed, or even hold your baby. *Try not to take it personally.* Besides, your wife is a new mother—cut her some slack. Just tell her, "Honey, I know that you are better at this than me, but I need to be able to do this my own way. I promise it will be fine." Try not to give in to the instinctive male response that says, "Fine, if you don't like the way I'm doing it, you can do it yourself!" This is not what we're trying to accomplish.

Be Patient and Keep Your Perspective

The other advice I've got for you is to keep your perspective. I know it feels like you've lost your wife. Don't worry—it's temporary. Let her be somewhat obsessive and preoccupied for a while. It will get better. She won't ignore you forever. It's a great time to put "money" in the bank by following the adage, "It's better to give than receive." Many experts in this field talk about an emotional bank account, which is the intangible (but very real) depository for all positive emotions that exists between a husband and wife.

When someone does something for the other that results in good feelings, it's like a deposit into the account. When you screw up, it's a withdrawal. The intimacy that exists between a husband and wife (which, by the way, will translate later into sex, so it's pretty important) is determined in large part by the deposits that have accumulated into the emotional bank account. This is a great time to invest! Each time you offer to lighten the load or do something for her, it's a deposit. Good things are happening in your relationship.

No Mom Is an Island

One of the things that new moms tell me is a big challenge for them is the feeling of being disconnected from the adult world. This is particularly true for women who leave careers to stay home with their baby. My advice to you is to make sure you encourage and support your wife's need to stay connected with her female friends. In a selfish way, this will benefit you. For one thing, she'll have someone else to vent to besides you (that's what we call a win-win scenario). Furthermore, you simply won't be able to fulfill all of her needs for adult contact and conversation. Therefore, she may begin to see you as not giving her enough of what she needs. Her friends can provide a good bit of her need for adult conversation and contact. Finally, hearing that other moms are or have struggled with the same hassles, worries, and frustrations will normalize them for her and help her to maintain a perspective. When moms get together, they share "war stories," which helps them feel less alone and normalizes the hard aspects of the parenting journey.

At times, some of your wife's friends may complain about their husbands, who aren't helping out as much as you are. When your wife hears this, it only makes your stock go up! Make sure you really support and encourage her need to connect with her friends. Of course, she can't do that unless you are willing to take over with the baby while she's doing this. Yes, there are mother's morning out programs, moms and tots, and many others, but these aren't the same as going to lunch, dinner, or whatever it may be with the girls. To be honest, I think the fact that it is good for her is reason enough; however, you get the added bonus of knowing that your wife will usually return from such an outing with a better disposition. Again, this is a win-win situation.

Dads should also be aware of a rather common condition known as the "baby blues," which is a mild, temporary state of any one or a combination of emotions such as sadness, anxiety, moodiness, or irritability that may show up within the first two weeks following delivery and may last for hours or even days. This condition appears in about 58 percent of new mothers and usually gets better on its own after a short time. However, between 5 and 20 percent of new mothers suffer something much more serious known as postpartum depression (PPD) (Feeney, Hohaus, Noller, & Alexander, 2001; Lyles, 2002). This condition looks just like severe clinical depression (e.g., serious sadness, feelings of hopelessness, disturbances in sleep and appetite, a lack of motivation, difficulty enjoying anything, and possible suicidal thoughts or feelings). PPD doesn't necessarily get better on its own after a few days and may require medical attention. If you think your wife may be suffering from PPD, encourage her to talk with her doctor about treatment options.

The Secret Formula

Okay—here's the secret I promised to tell you. I recently saw a goofy commercial that makes me laugh every time I see it. It's a commercial for some kind of "male enhancement" product. The man who has purportedly discovered this product is shown with this permanent smile on his face. Whether he's at the office, on the golf course, or driving home, he has this Cheshire Cat grin on his face. He's then greeted at home by a wife sporting a similar grin. The commercial wants you to believe that if you buy this product, your sex life will transcend all earthly limits, and you and your wife will walk through each day in bliss. Yeah, right.

I don't know whether the product they are selling works or not. However, I do have a secret that few men seem to know which, if applied, will actually result in happier wives and husbands. You and your wife may find yourselves sporting this goofy grin throughout the day in spite of yourselves. Research has identified a subgroup of new dads who know the secret I'm about to share with you. These new dads:

- feel better about themselves and about their family relationships than other men who don't know about this secret
- have higher self-esteem than the men who don't know this secret
- describe (along *with* their wives) their marriages as more satisfying, their families more cohesive, and their parenting stress lower
- have more social support and fewer stressful events in their lives

What's the secret? It is simply this: These incredibly smart guys *take a significantly more active role in running their households and rearing their children than other new dads.* That's it. In other words, these men really get involved in feeding, diapering, bathing, and playing with their new babies. They also help arrange for sitters, take the baby out for outings, respond when the baby cries, pitch a load of laundry in the washing machine now and then, help with the dishes, run the vacuum, and do whatever else needs doing.

I know what some of you are thinking, *That's her job! I work all day and she stays home. The last thing I need to do when I get home from working all day is to do dishes and laundry and all of that. What the heck is she doing all day?* If that's your attitude, then I hope the reward of feeling that things are *fair* to you is enough. But the research shows that you will be less happy than the guy who is willing to pitch in when he gets home. You'll drive off to work on Monday morning with a scowl while you see the guy who is taking this advice arrive at the office with that big silly grin on his face. It's your choice, but I know what I'd do.

In addition to offering hands-on help, it is also important for your wife to experience emotional support from you. Now I know that *emotional support* isn't a term generally used on the golf course or in the locker room, so let me define it for you: *emotional support* means that you are complimenting her, encouraging her, and that she feels you can empathize with her feelings and experiences. Some researchers led by Dr. Tony Palmer (2003) from the University of North Carolina found that a new mother's perception of emotional support from her husband was directly and significantly related to levels of marital satisfaction. It's really not that difficult. For most men, it means saying out loud what you're already thinking—that you think she's beautiful and terrific, that you think she is doing a great job as a mom, that you see and appreciate her good qualities, and that you understand some of the challenges and difficulties that she faces day to day.

Conclusion

I told you I'd be brief. In summary, understand that the best chance your marriage has of being great after you become parents is to change along with your wife as she transforms into a mother. It won't be as natural and involuntary for you as it is for her. However, it is vital that you evolve along with her. The best way to do this is to get very involved in the day-to-day care of your new baby and to offer emotional support to her. The best-kept secret among new dads is that you and your wife will be happier and more satisfied to the extent that you pitch in and help at home and offer emotional support. In addition, there are tons of data to support the fact that your child will benefit greatly from your involvement and participation.

The men I know who take this approach have won the respect and affection of their wives. They actually don't become "whipped" like most of you fear will happen if you try it. On the contrary, their wives go out of their way to support *them* because they see their husbands as a primary source of support, and they very much feel taken care of by their husbands. That only causes them to feel genuine affection and love toward their husbands. And, yes, they have more and better sex than the other guys! Now if that doesn't make you want to do a load of laundry and give your wife a compliment, I'm afraid I can't help you.

7

"You've Lost That Loving Feeling"

What Happened to Sex?

I'd like to take this opportunity to welcome most of the men to my book. If you are typical of most men, someone (probably your wife) gave you this book, you skeptically opened it to the table of contents and saw a chapter on sex and turned right to this page. Don't worry—that doesn't make you perverted or abnormal, it makes you male. If you are a new dad, you are asking yourself, "Will we ever have a sex life again?" You may be thinking, *The doctor said we could start having sex again in about four to six weeks. It's been seven and still no sex—what's the deal?*

First, the Good News . . .

The good news is . . . you will have a sex life again, and it can be just as good, if not better, than before. The bad news is that you may have to wait a while. The data shows that frequency of sex declines for almost all couples in the early months of parenting. About half of all couples studied also described a decrease in the quality of sex as well as the frequency. I should mention that there are some couples who find that their sex lives are not significantly different. If you are reading this and you are one of those couples who may be thinking, "Gee, we must be weird because we're having sex just as much as before," don't feel that there's something wrong with you. In fact, you may be in the lucky minority, and the rest of us are just jealous! However, for the majority of couples, having a baby is hardly an aphrodisiac. There are many reasons for this disruption in your sex lives.

Many women have a difficult time with pregnancy and delivery. Some women need time to heal from an episiotomy or a C-section. Even when everything goes smoothly, having a baby, while a very natural and wonderful event, is pretty physically traumatic on a woman's body. Most heal with time and are fine, but the time it takes varies greatly from one woman to another. A good rule of thumb is that sex should never be painful for either partner. If you experience pain during intercourse, you should stop until after you consult with your doctor.

For some women, the changes in her body have caused her to feel much less attractive and sexy. For most women it is important to feel attractive and sexy in order to enjoy sex. For example, some women are self-conscious about the "extra skin" that is inevitable following childbirth. For some women, being pregnant was not an issue since they were "supposed" to look pregnant. However, after birth, there's not a baby in there, and they still have some extra girth or loose tummy skin about which they are self-conscious. For some women, there is embarrassment from the flow of breast milk when they are aroused. It's difficult for some women to feel sexy when lactating.

Another factor that has a negative impact on your sex life is the fatigue we mentioned earlier. Most couples go through a few months of serious fatigue after a baby enters the home. Even the easiest infants don't follow the sleep patterns of an adult, and disrupted sleep patterns are just part of the experience. I still remember the morning after the birth of my first son. I spent the night in the hospital with my wife and son. The nurse came in the next morning and asked how things were going to which my wife responded, "Fine, but we didn't get much sleep last night." I'll never forget the nurse's prophetic response, "Honey, you'll never sleep well again." She was being somewhat sarcastic, but there was some truth to her statement. Fatigue is a part of parenting, especially in the early months. You can only manage it—you can't make it go away.

In addition to fatigue, there's the impact of all the extra responsibility we discussed earlier (that's in chapter 3 for those of you who skipped straight to this sex chapter). Feeling this much added responsibility takes a toll on people. Because moms (according to the research) take on the majority of the child-care, this means that she frequently feels "tapped out" at the end of the day. Remember, the research shows us that women feel that the role of parent consumes more of their identity six months after the baby is born than it does for men. In addition, the part of self that is experienced as "lover or partner" decreases more for women six months postpartum than for men. Both new moms and new dads feel the part of self identified as "lover or partner" decrease when surveyed six months after the birth of their first child, but the women experience a much bigger decrease.

Many couples I've spoken with talk about how difficult it is to have sex when a baby is in the other room. Now this is typically mom's complaint. I'm convinced that many men could have sex on the fifty-yard line during halftime at the Super Bowl (in fact, this would be a real turn-on for some men). The biology of men and women is vastly different. Men become aroused much more easily and are often much less deterred from sexual activity by distractions. Most women, on the other hand, do not become sexually aroused as quickly or easily. In addition, sex is much more of a psychological experience for women than for men. Atmosphere and emotions are more relevant to a woman's sexual experience than to a man's. This is why the idea of a baby in the other room is more of a distraction and disruption for women. Most men will tell you, "I'll be able to hear if something is wrong; but until I do, I'm not going to focus on the fact that my baby is in the other room." A woman is more likely to "listen out" for the baby and to be focused on the fact that something "might be" wrong. This distraction will seriously affect most women's ability to participate in and enjoy a sexual encounter. This difference between men and women isn't going to change significantly. Even when kids get older, lots of dads could have sex with kids banging on the bedroom door asking for peanut butter sandwiches, while many moms would be mortified by the thought of continuing with sex while kids are calling for her. Neither of these is "wrong"—it is simply part of the myriad differences between the sexes. It is also a significant reason that many new moms never feel there is a good time to have sex. After all, when are they not "on call?"

Another factor that has a detrimental impact on the sex lives of new parents is the simple fact that they just don't have as much time to spend together. For most people, sex is an expression of feelings of intimacy. Intimacy is the result of positive feelings that each person has for the other, and these feelings are the result of an ongoing process of feeling connected with each other. In his book *His Needs, Her Needs*, Willard Harley very aptly describes this concept as a

Love Bank into which couples make deposits that result in feelings of romantic love. Let's face it, even if you didn't have a new baby demanding more of your time, if you and your spouse just started spending less time together (talking, sharing, interacting, etc.), the intimacy level in your relationship would probably begin to decline, feelings of romantic love would begin to diminish, and your sex life might suffer as a result. This is one reason it is important that *all* couples—whether you are childless, have a newborn baby, or have grown children—constantly make an effort to stay connected with each other. Intimacy is like a houseplant. It requires constant and ongoing attention: neglect it for too long and it will wither and die. On the other hand, give it the time, attention, and ingredients it requires on an ongoing basis and it will flourish.

It is difficult to know which of these factors has a more serious affect on a couple's sex lives than the others, and there are undoubtedly other factors that may negatively impact your sex life after a baby arrives. For example, some couples have infants with difficult temperaments or special needs, which only increases the challenges of parenting and may exacerbate some of the fatigue and other challenges that make finding time for each other difficult. The point is that most couples see a pretty sharp decrease in the frequency and quality of their sex lives after baby enters the fold.

And Now the Good News . . .

As I've said, all hope is not lost. Your frustration with the disruption in your sex life is normal and common. It happens to most of us and is only temporary. Most couples resume their sexual relationship after becoming new parents and find that the quality is still great. Until that happens, I do have some advice that may be helpful along the way:

Understand without Blaming

Hopefully, the reasons I have outlined above for the normal disruption in your sex life make some sense. I want to encourage you to understand that these are unavoidable circumstances and that no one is at fault. The worst thing either of you can do is to blame the other or to blame your baby. It's part of the journey. Relax and don't panic—things are going to get better. Avoid turning against each other during this already stressful transition.

Keep Your Perspective

It is important to avoid getting tunnel vision about this period of your life. Keep your perspective. Almost every couple goes through a sexual struggle after the baby arrives. Keep reminding yourself that it is normal and temporary. Even if you do nothing, things will probably get better without any intervention at all. However, I still think there are ways to make this time easier and to speed your recovery to normal sex again.

Rediscover Nonsexual Affection

Many couples who fall into a prolonged period (which is admittedly a subjective term) of sexless cohabitation find that they stop offering other forms of physical affection. There are several reasons for this. For example, when there is an unspoken tension around the fact that "we aren't having sex," there is some apprehension around who will initiate it first. Because there is often a fear of being rejected—usually a man's fear—he is hesitant to put himself out there. He may begin to withdraw all forms of physical affection so that he won't be misinterpreted. For example, if he gives his wife a hug and she tenses up or pushes him away because she feels he is trying to initiate sex and she is just not in the mood, this could be very hurtful for him. He may reason that it is better to just avoid it altogether. The result is a relationship with very little affection of any kind. For a woman, she may not want to give the wrong impression. In other words, she may not want her husband to think she is making a sexual overture if she cuddles up to him in bed—after all, she may want to cuddle, but sex is the last thing on her mind—so she may just suppress her cuddle urge. This can go on for a while until the relationship becomes temporarily void of all physical affection. Another reason that couples stop showing physical affection is that the absence of sex can lead to some resentment for one of both of the partners. This resentment can build up a wall, which can result in the withdrawal of physical affection.

There was a definite "coolness" between Tracy and Joe. I couldn't help but notice that they were sitting on opposite sides of the waiting area, each reading a magazine. They had some typical marital issues that had resulted in layers of resentment and a growing distance between then. Tracy sat as close to the edge of my large sofa as she could, and Joe left plenty of space between them as he took his seat on the other end. Tracy sat with her arms folded and leaned away from Joe the entire time. Joe sat straight and looked at me during the entire session. It struck me that they barely interacted. In an effort to make a point and break some of the tension, I provocatively said, "Tracy, I can open the window if you'd like so you can lean out and get even further away from Joe." They both nervously laughed, and we talked about how infrequently they actually touched each other. They had fallen into an unhealthy pattern. The irony is that both of them missed holding hands and hugging. However, neither of them knew how to break the impasse that seemed to exist between then.

I believe that nonsexual physical affection is very important to a marriage. If a couple is physically affectionate only when one of them wants to have sex, then even hugs or hand-holding can become unwelcome gestures if one person is not "in the mood." I want to encourage you to make hugs, nonpassionate kisses, hand-holding, massages, and other ways of showing such affection a daily and frequent part of your interactions with each other. For some couples, I recommend that they assume that these are *not* sexual overtures unless one person makes it clear that they want to have sex. While some people are uncomfortable about being this direct, I think that it is worth the effort to overcome your inhibitions. The confusion over interpreting whether something is a bid for sex can lead to all sorts of problems. Discuss with each other how you want to signal that you want to make love so that the signs are clearly interpreted. For Dana and me, we use the expression "intimate time" to let the other person know we are in the mood. For example, "Honey, I was kind of hoping we might have some intimate time tonight." Whether you call it "canoodling," "private dancing," or something else is not as important as the fact that both of you know what you are talking about. If you know that the likelihood of misinterpreting a bid for sex is low, there is greater freedom to liberally express affection in physical ways toward one another. The best part is that the more you and your spouse show nonsexual physical affection toward one another, the more likely you will *both* feel interested in sex more often.

Remember, Sex Is More Important on Mars Than Venus

By now, everyone on earth knows about Mars and Venus, i.e., John Gray's notion that men and women act, think, and feel differently about most things. Sex is certainly one area that men and women generally view differently. Again, let me state from the outset that there are no hard-and-fast rules here; there are always exceptions. However, for the masses, sex generally means different things to men and women. While I cannot quote from the scientific literature on this, over sixteen years of clinical work (and just hanging out with guys) strongly suggest that men do not have a well-developed ability to adjust to a long period of no sex in a marriage. We just haven't developed very good coping skills for long periods of sexual abstinence. Women seem to be much better at coping with a lack of sex for a prolonged time. I've heard women described as "sexual camels": just as a camel can go for ridiculous periods of time without needing to drink water, it seems that some women can go for long frustration-free periods of time without sex. It is almost as though a woman can just dismiss sex from her thoughts if she is not having sex. The reverse is true for most men. In other words, the longer the period of time a man goes without sex, the more of a preoccupation it becomes for him.

For women, it seems that sex is very connected to their emotional state. This is why women generally are not interested in sex if they feel hurt, angry, upset, or anxious. Most men, on the other hand, are happy to have sex regardless of their feelings. I'm betting that one day they'll develop some type of new neuroimaging technique (ways that the structures of the brain can be studied, such as an MRI or CT scan) that will isolate an area in the limbic system of the brain even more responsible for sex than the amygdala. I think that they'll find that it is four times bigger for men and has very few neuronal connections to the emotional areas of the brain. I predict that the same area of the brain in women will have numerous, thick bundles of neurons that connect it to the parts of the brain responsible for emotional responses. That's my theory, anyway.

The point is this: the husband is probably more upset by the lack of sex than the wife . . . much, much more upset. (Okay, dads, here's where I'm going to advocate for you like I promised I would in the chapter on dividing up chores). Moms, do you remember how I asked your husbands to really pitch in with taking care of your baby and the housework because of how important it is to you? Well (and you had to see this one coming), it's your turn. I believe that because of how important this issue is to most men, I recommend that you find ways to acknowledge and work on responding to his sexual needs during this period of time. Before you freak out, call me a "typical man," and throw my book across the room, I'm not suggesting that you should have sex every night or every time he paws at you. I'm just saying that it will be very helpful to your marriage if you understand that this is a pretty big deal to him and work together with him to find ways to help him feel less deprived. It's okay to get creative here—lots of men are okay if sex sometimes doesn't necessarily include intercourse. The most important thing to remember is that this area of your marriage has the potential to become a bigger deal than it has to. I once heard that when sex is good, it only feels like it makes up about 10 percent of the relationship, but when it is absent, it feels more like 90 percent of the relationship. Whatever you work out should feel acceptable to *both* of you, of course. I would venture to guess that just as it will make you happier if your husband is doing more housework and taking care of the baby than *he* would prefer to do if left up to him, it will make your husband happier if there is more sex in your relationship than there would be if left up to you.

Now dads, if you highlight what I just wrote and use it to beat your wife over the head with, you will not be helping your cause. If your wife feels coerced or "guilted" into having more sex with you, it won't be much of a solution. This only leads to resentment and further relationship problems. My desire in suggesting this is to help your wife to see the issue from the perspective of a man, and to consider *voluntarily* making some changes that may work for both of you. Dad, you can also help your cause here by helping your wife feel a little less overwhelmed by the daily tasks of mothering. For example, you both may decide that tonight's the night (for whatever you decide you want to call it). In this case, perhaps dad brings home take-out Chinese and takes over things after dinner so mom can take a bath or relax for a while to get herself in the mood. Working together always works best.

"I Feel Like a Woman . . ."

Some very wise women have helped me see that it is a good idea for new moms to protect their feminine identity. What I'm about to suggest could sound very sexist coming from a man. I promise that it is advice I've gathered from women (including my wife) regarding suggestions they said that they would share with new moms. For example, they have suggested that new moms do things to help themselves feel attractive. My wife says that since jeans aren't likely to fit well in the months following pregnancy, it is a good idea to buy a new top (taking advantage of some extra cleavage from full breasts), get a new hairstyle, or buy some sexy lipstick. The small things can make a big difference and help a woman feel attractive and feminine. I have also had many moms tell me how important it is for them to start exercising again. The physical benefits are numerous. It not only helps reduce stress, it helps moms to feel like they are getting back into shape sooner. Finally, moms have shared with me that losing their feminine identity completely to motherhood is problematic for dad (who feels neglected), for mom (who struggles with a loss of identity), and eventually for baby if it sets up a pattern of smothering or being overprotective as the child grows older. As you (mom) feel more in touch with your femininity, sex doesn't seem like such a foreign concept.

Anticipate

One thing you will probably have to get used to is sex on a schedule. Spontaneous, bodice-ripping sex on the kitchen floor on a whim may be a loss you just have to grieve. Many people find scheduled sex as appealing as a dental appointment. If you couldn't agree more, I want to ask you to reconsider this notion. First of all, it may be the only way you are going to have sex for a while. Besides that, it can be rather exciting. After all, the anticipation of a sexual encounter is part of the allure. I would suggest that you talk about scheduling some "intimate time" (or whatever you chose to call it) and work toward making this as fun as possible. You can think about it, talk about it, flirt with each other in anticipation of it—whatever you do, make it fun!

Sometimes Dana and I will send each other an email in the morning planning some "intimate time" for later that evening. I have to say that I'm in a more positive mood for the entire day. Looking forward to some special time in the evening can only improve one's outlook!

Take Control

One of the most frequent reasons cited by one or both people for the lack of frequency in sex is that they cannot find time to be alone. Some couples allow their children to sleep with them in the same room or even in the same bed every night. I've read and heard several spirited debates regarding whether or not this practice is healthy or unhealthy for a child's development. There seems to be no real consensus among experts regarding this debate, and I tend to agree that there are many other factors that determine a child's mental health that carry much more weight than whether or not the child slept in the same bed with his or her parents during the first few years. However, I can state emphatically that the health of your marital relationship will be compromised if you don't protect your marital bed from your children. Of course, there will be some nights when it's fine to let them crawl into bed after a bad dream or during a thunderstorm. It is also perfectly fine to let them sleep in your bed on special occasions, or to let one of them sleep with mom or dad alone for a special night if everyone agrees that this is okay. However, I would strongly discourage you from making it a habit to share your marital bed with your children as a regular practice. Simply cuddling together in bed as husband and wife can contribute to feelings of closeness and intimacy. Besides, if you do find yourselves looking for something to do with a little extra energy at the end of the day and a spontaneous moment to share some sexual intimacy presents itself from time to time, it is not going to happen if Junior is tossing and turning between the two of you.

Assuming you do take steps to make your bedroom an "adults only" area of your home, some people describe anxiety about "shutting themselves off" from their children in order to have intimate time. I want to strongly encourage you to make time for intimacy a priority. This can establish a precedent in your family while your children are at an early age. If you don't value your time and relationship as a couple enough to create time together, you can easily set up a precedent of making your marriage take a back seat to every need your child may have over the next eighteen (or more) years. Of course, I am not advocating leaving your children in a "dangerous" situation while you slip off to make love, but I do feel that getting your child out of your bedroom for a period of time is important.

"Skyrockets in Flight . . . Afternoon Delight"

Some of you may be young and energetic enough to save sexual encounters until the end of the day. However, most of you may find that there isn't much left to give after 7:00 p.m. You may find that early mornings or afternoons offer you the best opportunities for intimate time together. Naptime for baby is a great option. Be flexible regarding when the time is right. Besides, it may be easier to plan around things like naps or other events. If it is difficult for both of you to be available when naptime rolls around, first thing in the morning is a splendid time for sex. Typically, this is the time of day when both of you are the least fatigued—just make sure to do something about that morning breath before you start!

Lighten Up

I am convinced that keeping a sense of humor about things is one of the best ways of coping with just about any situation. Sexual issues in a marriage can become touchy and serious very quickly. Try to keep a sense of humor; however, try to stay away from sarcasm as an attempt at humor. I tell couples that sarcasm is a bit like very hot Tabasco sauce—a little at the right time is fine, but you can overdo it easily. The last thing you want anyone to feel is ridiculed or mocked. Keep things light and fun. I recall sitting at the kitchen table with Dana a few months after our first son was born. We were both physically exhausted after a particularly difficult and sleepless night. I made the comment, "Boy, it's been a while since we had sex." She replied, "What's sex?" I said, "It's what got us into this predicament in the first place." (It was actually sort of funny at the time. Of course, sleep deprivation can make anyone a little punch drunk). The shared laugh about the situation helped us avoid getting too frustrated from being exhausted and sexually deprived and prevented us from taking our frustration out on each other.

Handle Egos with Care

A lot of people begin to feel some real insecurity when there is a problem with the sexual aspect of their relationship. Consequently, I believe that it is vital to reassure one another during this time of inevitable difficulty in your sexual relationship. This will certainly be accomplished by increasing the amount of nonsexual affection in your relationship. However, it is also important to verbally reassure each other regarding your commitment and love for one another and to let each other know that you still "do it" for each other. This is a crucial time to consciously compliment one another. Acknowledge that time and energy are in short supply and make sex more difficult. At the same time, tell her she's still "hot" and tell him he still makes your heart beat faster. Talk freely about memories of favorite sexual encounters you've shared with each other. This is a bit like talking about favorite vacations—why enjoy them only once; memories are fun to experience together as well. Also, maintain your optimism and reassure each other that this disruption in your sex life really is just temporary. If you make this part of your relationship a priority (and you should) and if you work at it, you can find time and energy to keep the coals stoked until you find your rhythm once again and the flame is burning as hot as ever.

8

Friends and Family

How Having a Baby Affects
the Rest of Your Relationships

While this book is about how having a baby affects the relationship between you and your spouse, the truth is that having a baby affects every relationship you have in some way. Your parents and in-laws are now your child's grandparents, your siblings and your spouse's siblings are now aunts and uncles (everyone has a crazy aunt or uncle—don't panic), your friendships are going to begin to change, and the list goes on and on. It is very important that you and your spouse negotiate these inevitable changes *together*. I strongly recommend that you be proactive and work from the same page as you navigate through the evolution of your relationships with your friends and family. Here are some things to think about.

Meet the Grandparents—Parents and In-laws

When you and your spouse have a baby, your parents and your in-laws become grandparents. Depending upon the relationship you currently enjoy (or perhaps, endure) with them, this is either welcome news or something that you may view with fear and trepidation. With the increasing number of stepfamilies today, it can get quite complicated. Some couples may find themselves with up to eight adults occupying the grandparent or stepgrandparent role. (In order to avoid confusion, I will simply use the term *grandparent* to refer to any adult in your life who might occupy a grandparent or stepgrandparent role). Fortunately, you and your spouse ultimately get to establish the terms and boundaries that need to be in place to keep these relationships healthy.

To begin, it is important to understand that every family brings different expectations and traditions to the role of grandparent in a family. Hopefully, you and your spouse have discussed what you expect in terms of the level of involvement and input from each of your parents after baby arrives. If you have not discussed this issue, now is the time. Some couples welcome and encourage daily involvement from one or more sets of grandparents. I know couples who have one set of grandparents involved in the role of primary caretaker for a good part of each day. These couples rely on the physical presence of one set of grandparents to help with the hands-on care of their baby. There is certainly nothing wrong with this *as long as both you and your spouse agree on the arrangement.* On the other hand, I know some couples who have a set of grandparents who see their child only once or twice each year. In fact, I know some couples who have one set of grandparents very involved in the role of grandparent while the other set of grandparents is barely involved at all. There are simply no rules regarding the level of involvement of each set of grandparents.

There is really little discussion necessary when both you and your spouse welcome and accept whatever level of involvement each set of grandparents offers. However, it rarely works out this easily. Often, one of you wants or expects more involvement and is disappointed by the lack of involvement of one or more sets of grandparents, or you may feel that one or more sets of grandparents is intrusive and over-involved, and you are trying to figure out how to tell them to back off. This can present all kinds of tricky relationship dynamics.

The Not-So-Baby-Crazy Grandparents

Let's face it: some people just aren't baby people. They aren't really comfortable around babies, they don't know what to do with them, and frankly, babies just sort of get on their nerves. This doesn't make them bad people—they just aren't baby people. If one or more of your parents or in-laws fall into this category, try not to judge them too harshly. They may be fine grandparents once your child gets out of the baby stage. Then again, they may not be child people either; in fact, they may just not like people very much at all. There's not much you can do to change people like this. My advice is to love them and accept them the way they are. Resist harboring any resentment and anger toward them. It's important for you to grieve any preconceived notions you may have had about Rockwellian visions of loving and supportive extended families gathered around the Thanksgiving table, laughing at the latest story of how junior finger-painted the kitchen wall with cake icing. Some grandparents just aren't going to be enamored with your baby. Again, if this describes one or both of your parents, forgive them, accept them, and love them. Sure, it's a loss for all of you, but you can still create a happy and loving family with your spouse and your child (or children).

Some people feel the need to confront their parents (and/or stepparents) about their lack of involvement. Of course, this is your call, but let me offer you some advice before you give them both barrels. First, you may be experiencing some old issues you have with your parents from your childhood. For example, perhaps your parents weren't that involved with you when you were a child, and this is the perfect opportunity to confront them by using their lack of involvement with their grandchild. Not a good idea. If you need to discuss issues you have with them about the past, don't use the present as an excuse. The waters will get muddied quickly, and everyone will walk away more confused and angry. Second, make sure that you don't go into a confrontation with the hope and expectation that once they see how hurt or angry you are, they will fall on their knees, acknowledge the error of their ways, apologize, and offer to be your permanent babysitter every Saturday night until your child is sixteen years old. This doesn't even happen in the movies, much less in real life. More often than not, such confrontations are met with denial, defensiveness, and comments such as "You never did appreciate all we did for you." Third, whatever the level of or lack of involvement your parents may have with your child now or in the future, they are still your parents and your child's grandparents. It is tough having unresolved conflict with first-degree relatives. Try to work hard to release them from your expectations and learn to live and let live. Again, who knows what will happen in the future?

On the other hand, if you need to express your feelings to your parents as part of a *process to move toward forgiveness and acceptance*, there is a litmus test to check your motives. As long

146

as their response is irrelevant to what you say to them, you may be ready to share how you feel. In other words, if you share your hurt, disappointment, or anger, and your parents completely deny any responsibility, and you are still able to walk away feeling that you have forgiven and accepted them for who they are, and you will not harbor resentment and bitterness, then the discussion may not make things worse. You should know, however, that some people cannot be confronted about anything, and to do so could end or seriously damage any relationship you may have with them. Therefore, make sure that confronting them is the only way you can move toward forgiving them before you take this step. If you feel you are having a very difficult time with this, or you still aren't sure how you want to handle it, you may want to consider getting some counsel from some trustworthy older mentors or even consider some brief professional counseling to help you get some resolution more quickly.

If the not-so-crazy-about-babies person is one of or both of your in-laws we're talking about, it is important not to judge them. Understand that your spouse may be hurt or disappointed by their response to your baby and support your spouse as much as possible. I would not recommend that you confront your in-laws on behalf of your spouse. This rarely has a happy ending. In fact, you might end up having everyone (including your spouse) upset with you. Just accept the way it is and reassure your spouse that within your nuclear family, you will create the type of family life that you both decide is right for your family.

The Omnipresent Grandparents

Of course, there are some parents or in-laws that seem to feel that a pregnancy is an invitation to move in with you. These types of grandparents may expect to be involved in your life much more than you are anticipating and certainly much more than you want. I have heard of grandparents who feel that they should be consulted on what the baby should be named, how the baby should be fed, dressed, disciplined, and a host of other things. These types of grandparents believe that they clearly know better than you about how to raise a child, and they will not hesitate to let you know if you are doing it wrong. Of course, this is entirely inappropriate and needs to be addressed.

It helps to understand that the motive of this type of grandparent is actually good. They really do want the best for you and your baby (problem is—they think only *they* know what the best is). I always encourage people to understand that good motives can often result in bad outcomes and to give others the benefit of the doubt when addressing the issue.

With over-involved grandparents, you simply have to have some good boundaries. The quintessential book on this topic is (interestingly enough) titled *Boundaries* by Dr. Henry Cloud and Dr. John Townsend. This book will help you understand how to define healthy relationship boundaries clearly and offers advice on setting up and enforcing these boundaries. If you don't have time to read another book and want the bottom line on boundaries with grandparents, here it is:

A. Your child has only two parents. This means that you and your spouse have executive decision-making authority on every issue regarding your child. Anyone can offer advice, but you and your spouse ultimately decide what is best for your child.

B. All other family members must accept and respect Rule A.

Pretty simple, eh? The truth is that it really is this simple. You and your spouse must accept and assume ultimate responsibility for parenting your child. It is fine, and actually a good idea, to ask for and accept advice from a number of sources, including grandparents, pediatricians, pastors, friends, and others. However, you and your spouse own the final decision. You must get comfortable with this. If you have grandparents who have trouble accepting your role as the parents, I would suggest that you have a very direct and honest discussion with them about the need to honor your role as the parents. If they continue to ignore your requests, I would recommend that you lovingly tell them, "We know that you love our child as though she were your own. We would very much like for you to be a part of our lives. However, we cannot allow anyone to usurp our authority as parents. If you continue to disregard our role as the decision makers regarding our daughter, you will leave us no choice other than to limit your contact with her." Again, this needs to be done by the biological child or stepchild of the grandparent rather than the son-in-law or daughter-in-law in question whenever possible.

It is *essential* that you and your spouse agree before having a conversation like this. You must be a team and agree that there is a need to establish these types of clear boundaries before doing it. If you don't agree, go back to the chapter on conflict and communication and continue to discuss the issue until you come to an agreement. Some people have a low threshold for the involvement of other family members while others welcome and encourage a great deal of involvement. You and your spouse must first agree on what level of involvement you want each grandparent to have before you start enforcing boundaries. Remember, neither of you will be "right" about how much involvement is best—you simply need to come to an agreement that you can both live with.

Advice vs. Control

Make sure that you are able to receive advice from others without becoming unnecessarily defensive. As new parents, you will benefit from the wisdom and experience of others who have walked the parenting path before you. Avoid reacting to unsolicited advice like it is an effort to usurp your authority or to control you. Welcome input from others—this does not challenge or minimize your authority as the parent. If you take advice, make sure to let the other person know you appreciate it. If you decide not to take a piece of advice, learn to graciously acknowledge their care and concern, and to say, "No thanks." Just remember, there is a big difference between a grandparent offering advice and one who disregards your wishes or instructions. Only the latter type of grandparent requires a confrontation regarding boundaries and roles.

Getting to "Our"

I have seen many couples get into nasty discussions about "your" family and "my" family. These labels are very polarizing and don't work well in a marriage. I strongly encourage you to change "your" and "my" to "our" as much as possible—certainly when discussing family. Once you become a couple, you establish your nuclear family. Radiating outward from this is "our" extended family. Some people are comfortable enough referring to their in-laws as "mom" or "dad"; however, some are not. Try to refer to each set of grandparents as "our" family or by their name. Instead of asking, "Are your parents coming for dinner?" ask, "Are Jim and Carol coming for dinner?" I know this sounds like I'm splitting hairs, but I believe that the different tone this sets is very important.

I am a big believer that once you marry, you share just about everything. Anything you keep as "mine" or abdicate as "yours" can eventually come back to create a source of conflict. You can argue all day long about "my rights" and "my this or that," and you may even win your argument. Or you may insist that something is "his problem" or "her issue" that you want nothing to do with. However, the couples I know who see most things as something to be shared with their spouse seem to have the best relationships. Try to view all of your extended family members as part of *our* extended family. This will greatly minimize the perennial arguments about how many holidays we spent with "your parents," how much less we spent on "my mother's" birthday present, and the like.

Aunts and Uncles

For the sake of simplicity, you can substitute "sister" or "brother" for "grandparent" in the sections above and apply the same advice for them as well. Siblings will vary regarding how much attention and involvement they offer once you have a baby. Don't try to change other people. If you have siblings who seem to disappear after your baby is born, accept their decision not to get involved very much or help out after your baby arrives. There could be a number of reasons for their lack of involvement (e.g., jealousy, a lack of confidence in their skills with a baby, or simply a low threshold and tolerance for all things pediatric). It's not your job to figure this out or to fix it. Remember to try to live and let live.

On the other hand, as with some types of grandparents, there are occasionally those siblings who feel that they need to jump in the middle and tell you how you are supposed to parent your child. Good boundaries are essential with this type of sibling.

151

Remember, you and your spouse are the parents of your child. You and your spouse will naturally gravitate closer to one or more siblings for a variety of reasons (e.g., similarity with parenting philosophies or values, proximity, working together, kids of the same age, etc.). This is a natural process that happens to everyone. The most important thing to keep in mind is that you and your spouse need to agree on parenting decisions and present yourselves to your extended family members as a united parenting unit.

Holidays and Headaches

Inevitably, you and your spouse will have to work out where you spend holidays, who is invited, and so forth. Every couple has to find a solution that works for them. Some couples prefer to visit parents or other relatives during holidays. If they live in different cities, this may involve some type of rotation each year. Other couples have parents or other family members visit them during holidays. Again, depending upon the size of your home, the relationships between your in-laws, and the number of in-laws you have, this may involve one big, giant family gathering for the holidays, or it may involve some type of rotation schedule. There are as many different solutions for these situations as there are families. Remember that there is no right or wrong solution— except to believe that there is one. You and your spouse need to work together to come up with a solution that you both feel good about. In *His Needs, Her Needs*, Willard Harley calls this the "policy of joint agreement." He suggests that you continue to discuss and problem-solve these types of issues until you reach a solution that both of you enthusiastically agree with and support.

If you are lucky, your extended family will understand that it is difficult to divide time and will be gracious and accepting of whatever you and your spouse decide. If you are typical, you will feel all kinds of pressure, manipulation, and guilt from extended family (hey, we're all human). This is when you really need to be together as a couple and in agreement about your decisions regarding how to handle holidays, birthdays, and other such events.

Pay It Forward . . .

One final thought on grandparents: some day, that little bundle of yours is going to grow up, get married, and have children with someone else. That will make you the grandparents. I'm certain that you will want to be part of your child's life and part of your grandchild's life. It is always a good idea to think ahead a bit and ask yourself how you would like to be treated in that situation. Would you want to be included in important events, sent occasional pictures, remembered at holidays, and so forth? Of course you would! It's probably a good idea to remember that whole "sowing and reaping" thing—and to treat your grandparents the way you will want to be treated when you are one.

A Kuhnian Crisis—Family Style

When I was a graduate student, one of the first things we were taught is the theory of a philosopher named Thomas Kuhn. Simply put, he stated that a system of any kind (a country, a business, or a family) rocks along with a certain way they think, believe, and do things (a paradigm). Only when something happens that results in their way of doing things no longer working (a crisis) does the system change the way they think, believe, and do things. They find a new way (a new paradigm) that works better given the new set of circumstances until a new crisis presents itself, and so on and so forth.

When a family grows by adding a child, this represents an event that forces a system to reinvent itself. The way you interacted with extended family members in the past will have to change. This is not a bad thing; it is simply an inevitable aspect of changing and growing families. It is important to anticipate and accept this. Then, you and your spouse need to make sure that your new paradigm is one you create together. Any and all changes that you need to make regarding roles your extended family members occupy, the time you spend with them, and so forth need to be agreed upon by you and your spouse. Expect changes and adjustments to be part of the deal for many years to come.

What about Our Friends?

All of these changes may prompt you to say, "At least my friends will be the same." Well . . . not necessarily. Just as having a baby results in some pretty dramatic changes in your relationships with extended family, you will likely experience some shifts in your friendships as well. There are generally two different types of friendships you will be dealing with:

Welcome to the Club: Friends with Children

You probably have friends who are just ahead (or maybe quite a bit ahead) of you in the parenting journey. After you have a child of your own, you become part of the parenting club. Suddenly, your empathy level rises a great deal. You may feel a little guilty for all the times you labeled them "neurotic," now that you are twice as bad as they ever were! It's all a natural part of the process. You may find that you grow closer to some of your friends who are parents. After all, you are sharing a huge life experience together. Your values, priorities, and interests will be much closer than before. In fact, most of the change that takes place with your friends who have children is positive and consists of strengthening bonds and growing closer.

However, there is one word of caution I would offer regarding your relationships with friends who are parents. You will inevitably run into one or more issues about which you have very different ideas and philosophies. It could start early. For example, how important is it and how long should you breastfeed your baby? Should you spank your kids or use time-out? Or it could come later. For example, is it okay to let your kids interrupt you when you are on the phone, or do you insist that they wait until you are finished with your conversation? Do you let them believe in Santa Claus, or do you believe that you should always tell your kids the truth about everything? Is a public school education adequate, or do "good parents" sacrifice to send their children to private school?

Be advised, even with your closest friends, you will not always see eye-to-eye on some fundamental issues. This is a volatile area, since people can become very emotional about what they believe regarding how they raise their children. The best advice I can give you is to *acknowledge*, *accept*, and *respect* the differences in how you choose to parent. The reason this is important in a book on marriage is that you and your spouse must first agree on your parenting decisions, then support each other as you run into differences of opinion with your closest friends. These types of disagreements have the potential to cause some real tension in friendships. If you and your spouse have very close couple friends with whom these differences present themselves, it is important that you both agree to acknowledge, accept, and respect the different philosophies and parenting practices between you and your friends without letting those differences interfere with your friendship. There are some people who may let this significantly interfere with or even end a friendship. If this happens, it will be important that you and your spouse support each other and decide how you want to handle this type of conflict with your friends.

Friends without Kids

You probably still have them—either married or single friends who are childless (whether by choice or not). These friendships will change more than your friendships with people with children. Here are some things to think about.

Your childless friends will still believe that the earth revolves around the sun rather than your baby. I realize that for you, the reference point for the center of the universe has changed. Just don't expect it to shift for your friends. They may even be polite and act like it for a while, but deep down, their priority list and the things from which they derive significance and meaning haven't changed much.

The reaction to the birth of a friend's child varies greatly. For many, they genuinely share some of your joy and excitement. However, it is not uncommon for some jealousy to rear its ugly green head. This is particularly true if you have friends who have been trying to conceive and are having difficulty. If you have a friend who has miscarried, your new baby could be a very difficult issue to deal with. Be sensitive to these types of issues. If they want to talk about their feelings, this is obviously healthy. However, respect their choice not to talk about it if that is their decision.

With your childless friends, you may need to talk about the changes that are about to or have already occurred as you become parents. Some things that will affect your friendships include:

- *You will be less available than before.* The early stages of parenting require a great deal of time. There is very little time you don't feel "on call." As I have suggested, it is important that you and your spouse deliberately and consciously make time for each other. You may find that there is not as much time left over to socialize with friends. If you don't talk with your friends about the reason you are less available, your friends could easily misinterpret, misunderstand, and draw erroneous conclusions.

- *You will be more tired than before.* Fatigue is inevitable. If you are used to late-night get-togethers or phone calls with your friends, this may have to change.

- *You may be a bit preoccupied with your baby and with parenting.* Apologize in advance for monopolizing conversations with "baby talk." Even if you try to avoid doing this, you will not be completely successful. Having said that, try to consciously ask about your friends' lives. They still have jobs, issues, and other things that are of interest, especially to them.

- *You will be less spontaneous than before.* If you were one of those couples who called at 5:00 p.m. on Friday to get-together with friends for dinner at 6:00 p.m., this may be a big adjustment. When our children were very young, I used to joke with Dana that going to a friend's house for an afternoon was a task no less complicated than a MASH unit redeploying to a different location. There were diaper bags to pack, pack and plays to disassemble, car seats to negotiate, bottles and burping cloths to gather, and more!

157

I sometimes thought that it would be easier to just move than to go anywhere with the kids. If someone called with last minute plans, I would just laugh.

- *Your priorities and values will shift some.* Most new parents find that having a baby causes them to see the world differently. Some people become more interested in politics or religion, other people start to think about money differently, and so on. Expect some changes in your priority list. Your friends will say that you have changed, and they are right. However, this is normal. Life-changing events sort of ... change your life. Some friendships may dwindle and grow less close while others may grow closer. You cannot help changing, and you cannot force your friends to like the changes that occur.

Again, the main point here is to anticipate and discuss the types of changes that may occur when you become parents. Expect some of your friendships to shift a bit. You and your spouse should talk about this together and support each other through these changes. The great constant is that you and your spouse will go through this *together*.

9

When Worlds Collide

Establishing a Parenting Philosophy

It has been said that all marriages are cross-cultural. In other words, each person brings to the marriage different customs, beliefs, traditions, and philosophies, and these differences must be merged into a new family "culture." Some people have suggested that this is one of the main reasons "arranged marriages" are ostensibly so successful: the couple starts out with a great deal of consensus on very important issues. No one knows exactly why these types of marriages tend to be more successful than marriages in which each person chooses the other. However, it is a plausible hypothesis that in arranged marriages, the couple has been raised with similar values, traditions, and viewpoints on major issues, and thus there is less disagreement over these things than there is for couples who vary greatly in these areas. Shared perspectives can only increase compatibility and the feeling of cohesion between a couple. For those of you who picked your own spouse, rather than having him or her chosen for you, there are usually a lot of differences in ideology that must be worked out.

Working Out Our "Cross-Cultural" Differences

As embarrassing as it is to admit one's own issues, I can offer a very simple example from the first year of my marriage to illustrate the point. During the first few weeks of my marriage, I recall walking out of the bathroom and telling Dana, "Honey, you need to know that this is an over-the-roll household." You see, she had placed the toilet paper on the roller so that it dispensed under-the-roll. I gave her the benefit of the doubt the first few times, but this latest episode had caused me to believe that she must have placed it that way intentionally. It was just wrong! She gave me that look (which I've since seen several times) that said, *Are you kidding me?* and calmly replied, "If you want to change it, then change it, but I've got better things to do than worry about how I put toilet paper on the holder." It was one of those defining moments in any relationship. I realized that being married meant some traditions just weren't going to last, as I had neither the inclination nor the energy to constantly change the orientation of the toilet paper roll each time. One and a half decades later, I've evolved into a much more mature, less controlling, and reasonable human being. However, I still put the toilet paper on the right way when it's my turn!

There are thousands of different examples of this "culture crisis" from minor issues (e.g., my family always opened gifts on Christmas Eve and your family opened them on Christmas Day) to more significant ones (e.g., I was raised Catholic and you were raised Jewish). Some traditions and ideals are held very strongly, and the urge to defend them is great. When differences arise regarding an area that one or both of you feels very strongly about, it can result in some real tension and difficulty.

If you've been married any time at all, you have certainly experienced the challenge of knitting different traditions into one unique family quilt and have hopefully been able to successfully blend your individual traditions, beliefs, habits, and philosophies into your new marriage in a way that feels respectful and satisfactory to each of you. Becoming a parent will test your skills at doing this like few other issues. Due to many obvious reasons, you will have an enormous emotional investment in what you believe to be the right way to raise your child. Each of us has firm convictions based upon our own childhood experience about what is right and wrong when it comes to parenting.

For example, Kevin made a solemn vow that he would *never* make his son eat everything on his plate because his parents made him do this, and he was traumatized by the cruel teasing of peers for being overweight. His wife, Sandra, on the other hand, was also required to clear her plate in an effort to teach the principle of "waste not, want not." Somehow she remained svelte throughout her life and has learned the value of not wasting things. She believes her parents were right in their method, and she plans to do the same with her son. Who is right? What should they do when their son leaves half of his food on the plate?

It is essential that both you and your spouse vehemently avoid taking the position that you are "right" when it comes to a disagreement about parenting. Agree that you both love your child and that each of you wants only the best outcome. Accept the cold, harsh truth that you simply don't have all the answers yourself. You will be a much better parent with input from your spouse. Remember Dr. Gottman's research on happily married couples? One of the things that differentiates couples who stay together and are happy from the unhappy or divorced ones is that they "accept influence" from each other. In other words, in these happy households each person looks for the validity and value of their spouse's input and tries to allow this input to affect and influence the way they see and think about things. In most disagreements I witness between couples in my office, each person is spending all of his or her energy convincing their spouse that their own opinion is "more right" in an effort to influence the spouse to think like them.

This is exactly the antithesis of accepting influence, which is the process of investing energy into trying to allow your spouse's opinion and input to influence your own viewpoint. Again, you must avoid the belief that you have all the answers when it comes to parenting. Remain open and constantly strive to learn as a parent; value your spouse's opinion regarding parenting philosophies.

A classic example of a couple running into trouble with different philosophies regarding how to handle an issue is illustrated by a conversation in my office between Beth and Frank. They were the proud parents of seven-year-old Brian. A seemingly innocuous disagreement had escalated into a rather heated exchange that they brought into my office. Brian played in the local recreational soccer league. He was growing disinterested in team practices and told his mother that he did not want to go to practice on Wednesday. Beth thought this was perfectly fine—"After all, it's just a bunch of first graders running around in a crowd after a stupid ball! They don't even keep score. He's just a kid; what's the big deal?" Frank, on the other hand, was adamant about their son attending practice. "When you make a commitment, you keep it. Brian needs to understand that you can't be a member of a team and just show up when you want to. The team is depending on him to be there." The dialogue continued:

Beth: Come on Frank, you act like it's the Olympics or something. The team could care less if he shows up or not. He's a little boy and he needs some downtime.

Frank: I'm not raising a kid who becomes irresponsible and lazy. I played sports all through high school, and there are plenty of times I didn't feel like going to practice, but do you think I just stayed home every time I felt like it? No way!

Beth: Well, he's not you, and I don't want to turn him into some sports fanatic like you!

You can see how this kind of conversation is beginning to deteriorate and how Beth and Frank are engaging in the kind of destructive pattern of conflict that we discussed in chapter 2. It is essential here that they begin to understand the concern behind their positions instead of continuing to argue about who is right. Beth's concern behind her position was that Brian was being pushed too hard and needed some rest and downtime. The truth was that she also played sports in high school, and she wanted Brian to develop a love for athletics. She worried that if they pushed him too hard, he would burn out at a young age and not continue with organized sports as an adolescent. Frank's concern was that Brian would turn into an irresponsible kid who would give up when things got boring or difficult. He wanted Brian to learn to finish what he started and to take his commitments seriously. Once we got the real concerns out in the open, it was much easier for both Beth and Frank to validate each other's concerns and to work together to come up with a solution that took both of their very valid concerns into consideration as they reached a decision that each of them could support.

In this case, Beth agreed that for the remainder of the brief season, she and Frank would require Brian to attend all practices and games. She understood and validated how important it was for Frank that Brian showed a commitment to his team and his decision to play. However, they agreed to carefully consider how many and what type of activities to allow Brian to participate in from then on. Frank was able to validate that pushing Brian too hard at a young age would likely result in burnout, and Brian could very easily end up trying fewer activities if they made extracurricular activities too serious while he was so young. They also agreed that they needed to continue to talk about this issue more as future decisions needed to be made. This is a very healthy awareness, as many of the same disagreements need to be addressed and worked through several times as circumstances and situations vary. Had they continued to focus their energy on being "right" and defending their position, they would have walked away without a mutually agreed upon solution and would have succeeded only in attacking and criticizing each other, which would have decreased their positive feelings for each other.

If you run into an ostensible impasse with your spouse, look over chapter 2 and keep discussing the area of disagreement until you can reach some compromise or decision, even if only temporarily. For couples who really get locked down on this issue and feel like it is too much work to reach agreements regarding parenting philosophies, I usually point out that if they were to eventually divorce, they would give up all decision-making rights to their spouse when the child is with the spouse. I then ask them, "Which would be easier: continuing to work together to reach agreements or getting divorced and having no influence at all in this area that you obviously feel very strongly about and letting your spouse have 100 percent decision-making authority for half of the time?" It's a harsh truth, but it makes the point.

If you end up having more than one child, or if you have more than one child already, you will learn that children come out of the womb hardwired differently. I once heard psychologist and author Dr. Wendy Mogel say that being a parent is a bit like being given a package of unlabeled seeds. Our job, as parents, is to plant the seed and make sure that they get plenty of the things that allow them to grow and then to step back and see what God has given us to raise. I believe she is right. Our children's personalities and temperaments certainly are influenced by our actions as parents; however, the vast majority of who they are was predetermined by God before we first held them in our arms. Because of these differences, it is important to realize that an effective parenting style for one child may prove completely ineffective for another, even within the same family. Some children require and do better with firmer discipline, which could cause another child to wither like a delicate flower in the desert sun.

One example of this difference in temperaments occurred in my home recently. Dana and I had some of our friends over for dinner. All of us have children between the ages of four and twelve years. Some of the younger children were doing what young children do: running around the kitchen chasing each other. One of the dads very calmly stated, "Hey guys, please stop running in the kitchen." One of the boys dissolved into tears and headed straight for his mother's lap (the more sensitive type), one simply stopped and went outside, and the other two continued to dance into the living room, where the running resumed (the concrete thinkers—after all, he said not to run in the *kitchen)*. This difference in temperaments and personalities is another reason that it is important to work together with your spouse to come up with a parenting philosophy that you can agree is best for this particular child in this particular situation. When it comes to parenting children, there are few "one size fits all" approaches.

The Basics

Suggesting a specific parenting paradigm is beyond the scope of one chapter in a book. In fact, the bookstore is filled with books on just that topic. To help you get started, however, let me suggest five basics that can help you draft your own parenting model. Think of these five ideas as the framework upon which you build your philosophy together.

1. Establish your few nonnegotiable rules first.

You and your spouse should agree on what is simply nonnegotiable (e.g., no hitting, no name-calling, no destroying property, etc.). Keep these limited. Remember, it is better to have fewer rules/limits in place that you will actually enforce rather than a long list of rules you rarely or inconsistently enforce.

2. Agree on how you will enforce rules.

You should talk about the forms of discipline you will use (e.g., corporal punishment, time-out, positive reinforcement, a combination of methods, etc.). This can be a hotly debated topic. Remember that even professionals disagree on which methods are best. The important thing is that you and your spouse choose a method of rule enforcement that you can both support and enforce consistently.

3. Remember that discipline is an important but small part of parenting.

You must discipline your children. However, you will spend much more time providing love, instruction, guidance, support, and nurturance to them. Spend the majority of your focus on these more positive aspects of parenting.

4. Keep your perspective—don't catastrophize.

It is easy to make mountains out of molehills. Don't let a minor issue escalate into a catastrophe. If you and your spouse are at odds over a particular issue, decide how important it is in the big picture of things. Chances are good that on many of the issues about which you disagree, there are no significant long-term outcomes for your children that will be determined by how you decide to handle the issue. Avoid getting tunnel vision on issues.

5. Finally, stay flexible in your parenting approach.

Your children will grow and develop quickly. You will probably find that as soon as you decide on an approach for one stage of development, you will be forced to revise it because it will no longer fit for your growing child. After all, will you still worry about what to do if your child is biting his classmates when he is a sophomore in high school? I hope not! This is another good reason not to get stuck on one certain issue or way of handling it—such things will almost certainly need revision soon.

Remember, two heads are definitely better than one when it comes to parenting your child. Embrace and welcome the different ideas your spouse brings to the parenting table. Work together to come up with an approach to parenting that you can agree on and implement together. Refuse to allow different ideas about parenting to divide and conquer your relationship. After all, no one has the best interests of your child in mind more than you and your spouse.

10

Juggling on a Tightrope

Special Issues with Stepfamilies

"What about Us?"

If you and your spouse are raising children in a stepfamily, most of what you have read in this book may sound as though it has been written to first-time married couples only. On the contrary, all of what I have written is applicable to stepfamilies. It's just that you have more complex challenges than couples in a first marriage. You may be thinking, *If only it were as easy as working out household chores, conflict, and sex, we'd have it made. That's easy compared to dealing with ex-spouses, visitation schedules, and all the rest.* Indeed, the choice to become a member of a stepfamily is a serious commitment and is a choice to take on significant challenges. The good news is that there are some terrific and happy stepfamilies, and you can make it work!

169

If you are a member of a stepfamily, you are far from being alone. Obtaining hard data on stepfamily statistics is difficult. The U.S. Census Bureau acknowledges that "Census 2000 may have identified only about two-thirds of all stepchildren living with at least one stepparent because of the manner in which the data were collected" (*U.S. Census Bureau 2000*). We do know that most people who divorce will eventually remarry, and most of these remarriages involve children. Some statistics predict that over half of all people will live in a stepfamily at some point in their lives. It is believed that soon, if not already, stepfamilies will outnumber intact, nuclear families. Therefore, it is important to address the specific challenges that face this very important and sizeable group of families.

A Family by Any Other Name . . . Is Not the Same

First, let's get the term straightened out. A stepfamily is defined as a family in which one or both adult partners have children from a prior relationship. From my work with and research about stepfamilies, the term *stepfamily* is preferred over the more media-popular and politically correct term *blended family*. The term *stepfamily* is preferred because the term *blended family* sets up unrealistic and potentially harmful expectations for the stepfamily. The truth is that unlike the outdated but well-known, quintessential, television stepfamily the Bradys, the vast majority of stepfamilies do not "blend" into one coherent primary family. There are always connections and significant relationships for the children in stepfamilies that predate and extend far beyond the new stepfamily. To try to force the new stepfamily into a single, close-knit primary family that looks and functions like a nuclear family typically sets everyone up for frustration and failure. If you are contemplating becoming a stepfamily or if you already are one, you have to accept that your stepfamily was preceded by another one, and divorce doesn't terminate or minimize these relationships. Children will not decrease the love and feelings they have for nonresident parents, nor should they be expected to!

When I shared with my business partner and colleague, Dr. Michael Lyles, the news that I was "finally" getting married, he made a statement that I never forgot. With a professorial gaze, he looked at me and said, "You know, marriage is God's way of getting to all of your personality flaws that he can't reach while you're single." Those words still ring in my ears today. Borrowing from his wisdom, I would say that being a member of a stepfamily is God's way of sanding off any rough edges that the sculptor's chisel of prior marriage and divorce may have missed.

Obviously, one chapter of a book cannot begin to adequately address all of the challenges that are unique to a couple in a stepfamily. Nevertheless, here are some of the more common challenges to stepfamily couples that I see in my office:

1. Great Expectations—Dispelling the Brady Myth

Although *The Brady Bunch* was a popular show, it was a terribly unrealistic portrayal of life in a stepfamily. First of all, they had a full-time housekeeper (who was always cheerful no less)! There were no nonresident spouses to deal with, no visitation schedules, and no significant discipline issues. Now, I don't think anyone who becomes a stepfamily really expects life to be like the Bradys', but I do think that some people have unrealistic expectations about how things will develop once the stepfamily forms.

It is vital that you and your spouse expect everyone to adjust to a new stepfamily on different timetables. Each child in a stepfamily has different experiences which affect how they adjust to stepfamily life. Such variables include how long it has been since the divorce, how the biological parents get along postdivorce, how much time they had to get to know the new stepparent before remarriage, whether they had to live with new stepsiblings, whether they have to move or change schools, and so on. All of these and many other things affect how children will feel about and adjust to the new stepfamily. As an adult, you must be willing to give the children in a stepfamily time and support as they make these substantial adjustments in their lives. Do not expect children to embrace a stepparent with open arms. It's great if this happens, but it is not typical. Everything will have to be worked out over time including schedules, rules, discipline, visitation, who doesn't like lasagna: you name it—it's something that everyone has to adjust to. In an effort to set up realistic expectations, consider the following:

- Expect a long period of adjustment.
- Expect everyone (including the adults) to make sacrifices and compromises.
- Expect your feelings for your biological children to always be stronger than your feelings for your stepchildren (even though you don't have to let this determine how you *treat them*). You will always have feelings for your biological children that are unparalleled by any other relationship. You need to accept that while you may grow to genuinely love your stepchildren, you will probably love them in a different way than you love your biological children. The same holds true for your spouse if he or she is a stepparent to your children. You can treat them all fairly and show them all affection and such. However, you will probably be disap-

pointed if you expect the feelings of a stepparent toward a stepchild to be the same as the feelings a biological parent has toward a biological child—whether we're talking about your feelings or those of your spouse.

- Expect to have to share—a lot.
- Just like *any* family, expect to keep working on things from now on. All families have to commit to each other and work together. It is possible to have a healthy and happy stepfamily if you are willing to work at it and if you don't set yourself up with unrealistic expectations. After all, even nonstepfamilies are stretched to the limit at times. Why expect stepfamilies to be any different?

2. Who am I?—Work with your spouse to define the role of stepparent in your stepfamily.

Research on stepfamilies reveals something interesting regarding how each member views the role of stepparent. One study asked parents, stepparents, and stepchildren about the ideal way a stepparent should relate to his or her stepchildren. Most of the adults (about half) responded that the ideal role of a stepparent is best described as a "parent." The terms "stepparent" and "friend" were chosen as a description of the ideal way a stepparent should relate to his or her stepchildren by less than one-fourth of all of the adults. Stepchildren had a different response to this same question. Forty percent of stepchildren chose the term "friend" to describe the ideal way a stepparent should relate to them. Only 29 percent chose the term "parent" and 18 percent chose the term "stepparent."

These data suggested that most adults expect to assume the role of another parent to a stepchild in a stepfamily. However, most stepchildren do not share this expectation. It is important that you and your spouse discuss carefully what your role with the stepchildren will be, assess how realistic this role is initially, and agree on the final decision. In my experience, it is disastrous for a stepparent to charge into a newly formed stepfamily with the expectation that stepchildren will see them as another parent. Many stepchildren struggle with some significant issues that may make it difficult to embrace a person in the role of their biological parent. There also may be a fear that if they get too close to you, they'll be hurt. (After all, their biological parents got divorced—why should they believe this marriage is any more likely to last?) If you are a stepparent, be patient with stepchildren and their process of figuring out what your role in their life may be. Here is some advice:

- *Don't make a big deal out of what they call you.* Discuss and agree on a term that feels respectful and genuine (e.g., your first name, stepmom or stepdad, etc.). While some (usually younger) stepchildren may want to call you "mom" or "dad," *never* insist that they refer to you by these titles. It is possible that what a stepchild calls a stepparent may evolve over time as the relationship evolves. However, this must be the stepchild's choice. It should also be acceptable if different stepchildren refer to stepparents by different names. For example, six-year-old Jay may refer to his new stepfather as "dad" while Jay's thirteen-year-old-sister, Susan, cannot bring herself to call anyone "dad" except her biological father. This is fairly common and should be accepted by the adults involved. On the other side of the coin, if six-year-old Jay comes home from visiting his nonresident father and refers to his new stepmother as "mom," he should not be chastised or made to feel badly about it.

- *Leave the discipline to the biological parent at first.* This does not mean that a stepparent has no position of authority in a stepfamily—it just means that the stepparent is not the primary enforcer of the rules. Children are accustomed to having adults in their lives who occupy positions of authority (e.g., teachers, aunts, uncles, coaches) but who don't necessarily serve as primary disciplinarians. Understand that there is a big difference between "parenting" and discipline. Parenting involves loving, supporting, caring for, nurturing, and setting limits, to name a few. Discipline is only one small part of parenting which refers to enforcing the consequences of violating rules. This small part should be carried out by the biological parent initially.

- *Don't try too hard.* Many new stepparents make the mistake of "courting" the stepchildren in an effort to get the children to like or accept them. This usually comes across as phony and manipulative. Just be yourself and let them accept you on their own terms.

- *Be flexible and patient.* Allow the relationship to evolve over time.

3. The "Ex-Factor"—Accept the fact that your spouse was married before the two of you married.

If you marry someone who is divorced with children, you had better get used to the idea that your spouse will be communicating with his former spouse on a regular basis. In my experience, this is typically most difficult for women who are entering a first marriage to a man who is divorced. Let me just put it to you straight: the ex-wife is not going to disappear just because you married her ex-husband. Of course, spouses of either sex can have trouble with this issue. I just see more women struggling with this issue than men. If you can't handle your spouse talking with his or her ex-spouse, you are going to be miserable living in a stepfamily.

It is very important to understand that you should and must accept your spouse's relationship with his ex-spouse if they have children together. The research on divorce and children is extensive. One factor upon which all the experts agree (and it's tough to get experts to agree on much) is that the best way to protect kids from the negative effects of a divorce is for the parents to establish and maintain a cooperative co-parenting relationship following the divorce. This means that after the divorce, they stop fighting each other and work together cooperatively for the sake of the children. As the saying goes, "There are no ex-parents, only ex-spouses." Your stepchildren need your spouse and his ex-spouse to have a cooperative relationship with one another.

The data on remarriage indicates that remarriage typically affects the co-parenting relationship negatively. There are many factors for this. For example, Cindy and Scott divorced with two children. Scott remarried Jennifer, who has never been married. Factors that may negatively affect Cindy and Scott's co-parenting relationship as well as Scott and Jennifer's new marriage include:

- Cindy is jealous of the fact that Scott found someone and remarried before she did.
- Cindy may feel threatened by Jennifer, especially if her children seem to like Jennifer.
- Jennifer, having never been married, may feel jealous of the relationship Scott had with Cindy, and she may put pressure on Scott to minimize or avoid contact with Cindy.

Whenever Cindy calls Scott to discuss an issue with the children, Jennifer becomes cold and distant toward Scott.

- Cindy and Scott now have to travel much further to arrange drop-offs and visitations because when Scott married Jennifer, he moved across town to be closer to Jennifer's job. Furthermore, arranging schedules regarding the children's activities is more difficult because Scott now has to consider Jennifer's schedule when planning ahead. Cindy has very little interest in accommodating Jennifer's schedule, therefore discussions between Cindy and Scott about scheduling are tenser, and compromises are found less often.

- Jennifer is livid every time she sees that big child support check that Scott writes to Cindy. She secretly thinks, *She doesn't even spend all of that on the kids! Imagine what we could do with that extra money each month!* Consequently, she has a difficult time feeling and acting positively toward Cindy, and she has difficulty when Scott is nice to Cindy on the phone or in person.

There are countless reasons that remarriage may negatively affect the quality of the co-parenting relationship between divorced parents. However, it is extremely important that ex-spouses work together to maintain a good co-parenting relationship, and it is important that the new stepparent support this relationship enthusiastically. In a perfect world, all the adults (biological and stepparents) work together and form a "parenting coalition" for the sake of the children and stepchildren. Very mature and committed parents and stepparents are able to do this. However, it also works well if the new stepparent simply accepts and supports the co-parenting relationship between her spouse and the ex-spouse.

No child chooses for his parents to divorce. I believe that it is the responsibility of adults to minimize the difficulty that a child must endure following the breakup of the family. Therefore, allow me to say this to you bluntly: if you feel threatened by or jealous of your spouse's ex-spouse, get over it. This is your problem, and you need to work on it. It is incredibly selfish of you to expect your spouse to discontinue or minimize his or her co-parenting relationship with your stepchild's other parent because of your insecurity. If you accept and support the co-parenting relationship between your spouse and his ex-spouse, you will earn the appreciation of your spouse and your stepchildren, you will make the most significant contribution possible to the overall adjustment of your stepchildren, and you maximize the chances of success in your stepfamily.

4. Getting more pieces out of the pie—allocating finite resources

Time, money, physical energy . . . all of these are finite resources for an individual or a family. In other words, once you run out, you're out. Successful couples in a stepfamily must learn to budget all finite resources. I observed earlier, based on my experience with stepfamilies, that more women than men have trouble accepting and dealing with the presence of an ex-spouse. The issue I find more men struggling with is the idea of assuming some or all of the financial responsibility for their stepchildren. There may be some resentment or anger that the biological father is not "doing his part." Many stepfathers feel taken advantage of if they have to step in and provide financially for a stepchild if a biological father is delinquent or negligent with child support payments or if the stepfather feels that his spouse did not get a "fair settlement" during her divorce. This issue is best discussed *before* marriage but, like many issues, may not arise until after the "I do" part. In any event, just as I believe that a stepparent must accept the presence of an ex-spouse for the sake of a child, I believe that a stepparent must be willing to accept some financial responsibility for a stepchild. There are, of course, innumerable different issues to which this could apply, and each one should be discussed and worked out. However, it is unreasonable for a stepparent to feel that he or she will have no financial obligation or responsibility to a stepchild.

Time is one of the most precious commodities for a stepfamily. One of the most frequent complaints I hear from couples in a stepfamily is that there is no time for "us." In other words, kid activities, visitation commitments and obligations, and the desire of biological parents to spend individual time with their biological children in order to prevent them from feeling as though they have "lost" their parent to their new stepparent all decrease the amount of time available for the new couple to spend together. The only way to manage this situation effectively is through deliberate and conscious planning. Stepfamilies must get used to the idea that their time has to be scheduled in advance. I recommend that all families take a few minutes (or more, if needed) on a Sunday afternoon and look ahead to the coming week. Everyone should list their commitments and activities and plan for these. Then, planned family and couple time needs to be scheduled into the week. Of course, things come up that are not anticipated and force families to be flexible, but without a plan, you're in trouble.

Even stepfamilies who plan complain that there's little time for the couple to spend together. I try to remind them that they probably dated before they got married and then ask them how they managed to pull that off. Inevitably, they tell me that many of their "dates" were around the activities of the children. For example, Joe was so in love with Sarah and her son, Jake, that he was happy to spend time with Sarah at Jake's baseball game on Saturday afternoon. Just being able to spend time with her was all that mattered. They actually were able to have meaningful talks while watching her nine-year-old son play baseball, and they were as affectionate as being in public allowed. It was a time to connect. The fact that Joe was willing to meet with her around Jake's games made her fall that much more in love with him, and Joe didn't seem to mind finding romance in a Little League park. Every now and then Sarah was able to comfortably get a sitter so they could go on an "adult date night," but they were happy to spend time together whenever and wherever they could. I remind couples that the only thing that has changed since the dating phase of their relationship is their expectations. Why not continue to connect and spend time together during kids' activities? Why not occasionally find a sitter and go out on an adult date? If couples were able to spend enough time together to decide to get married when they lived in separate homes, surely they can find enough time to spend together to stay married now that they live under the same roof! It is really a matter of challenging unrealistic expectations and resetting priorities.

5. Don't forget the grandparents.

Many children form special and wonderful relationships with their grandparents. It is my opinion that the presence of a loving grandparent in a child's life is a dramatically undervalued thing. Many children I talk with speak adoringly about their grandparents and feel a tremendous loss when they lose one. Divorce and remarriage often derails these relationships. Unfortunately, too many couples fail to appreciate the need to value and support them. As we've discussed, time is a precious commodity. Don't forget to honor, support, and make time for grandparents with whom the child has a meaningful relationship. Again, this requires stepparents to support the spouse's relationship with a spouse's former in-laws.

6. One of our own—having a mutual child within a stepfamily

The decision to have a child together is one of life's most important decisions. The commitment is lifelong and life-changing. Having a mutual child in a stepfamily is also an important decision to consider. As we've said, every stepfamily is different: some stepfamilies are formed by two adults, both of whom have children, while others are comprised of one adult with children and one without. For the latter stepfamilies, it is not uncommon for the spouse who has no biological children to want a child of his or her own. Often, this produces a feeling of obligation for the other to fulfill his or her spouse's dream of having a child. Even for stepfamilies formed when both adults have children from prior marriages, spouses sometimes feel the need to "solidify" their relationship by having a child of their own.

The research on this issue is not vast. However, some limited studies show that having a mutual child can have a positive as well as a negative effect on a stepfamily. For example, some parents report that having a mutual child had a positive influence on their relationship with their *stepchildren*. Perhaps seeing the stepparent as their half sibling's parent changed the way they viewed their stepparent. On the other hand, older stepchildren commonly saw a new child as an undesirable addition to an already complicated life. There is no way to predict the effect of a mutual child on a stepfamily. One thing is certain, however: no couple should have a child unless *both adults enthusiastically agree that they are ready.*

I cannot say this strongly enough. This is a true statement for first-time couples as well as for couples in stepfamilies. In one study (Cowan & Cowan, 2000), if a husband was resistant to having children and the wife became pregnant, the results were disastrous—all couples were divorced by the time the child was six years old. I don't know of a similar study on stepfamilies, but I do not expect that the results are more positive. *Never* pressure your spouse to have a child if he or she is not ready. Likewise, *never* agree to have a child if you are not ready. It is fine to discuss the issue and express your feelings, but don't manipulate, withdraw, or pout if your spouse is not as ready as you are. It is best to wait or even to not have a child together at all rather than to bring a child into the world if one of you does not really want to. The effects of pressuring a reluctant spouse to have a child are almost always negative, and are often fatal to the marital relationship.

If you and your spouse agree *enthusiastically* that you want to have a mutual child, consider the impact upon stepchildren. You don't need their permission, but you should be aware of their feelings, that they may be jealous, anxious, or otherwise distraught. Try to reassure them realistically. For young children, explain that your love is not like a pie that must now be cut into smaller pieces to feed more people. Instead, you bake a separate pie for each child—children have to share things like toys and space in the house, but your love for them is special and *all theirs*. For older children, listen empathically to their fears, anxieties, and concerns. Try to problem-solve together and address their questions and concerns respectfully.

7. What about adoption?

There may be situations that raise the question of adoption in a stepfamily. In other words, should the stepparent adopt the stepchild? There are several circumstances that may cause a couple to consider this option. For example, one biological parent may be deceased and the other remarries. Another circumstance that may cause a stepfamily to consider adoption is one in which the nonresident parent is not present or involved in the child's life. Some couples feel that having a stepparent adopt a stepchild can offer the experience of having an intact nuclear family for the child as well as for the parents. In addition, adoption can eliminate some confusing issues such as a stepchild having a different last name from the parent (e.g., when a biological mother assumes the name of her spouse), stepparent, and any future half siblings.

The decision to adopt a stepchild is a significant one which may depend upon many factors. There are few empirical studies of adoption within stepfamilies. The few that exist indicate that adoption within stepfamilies is considered most when there is a particularly close relationship between stepfamily members and these stepfamily members want their relationships to be recognized. I have had some experience with adoption and the process of considering adoption within a stepfamily. Based on this experience, I would like to offer some advice regarding this issue.

The most important first step is to make sure that the biological parent, stepparent, and child agree that they want to pursue adoption of the stepchild by the stepparent. There should be 100 percent agreement and enthusiasm on this point. Of course, if the child is too young to understand or discuss this issue, then the child's agreement is not a factor. After all stepfamily members agree, make sure that if the nonresident parent is alive, there will not be significant opposition (particularly a legal challenge) to efforts to adopt. If a nonresident parent does not want to relinquish parental rights, I would strongly caution you to reconsider pushing this issue. Children do not typically benefit from being in the

The Journey Continues

Final Thoughts

If, as Tom Cochran sings, "life is a highway," then the road forks many times on life's journey. As you travel through the years with your spouse by your side, life will present you both with many situations that will force you to redefine yourself and your relationship. At times, these forks in the road will be unwelcome and difficult, but at other times, these forks will mark the most joyous and celebrated events in your life. Some of these forks in the road are easy to see and are even self-imposed while others come with little or no warning and are not the result of choices you make. The forks in the road themselves have less to do with where you end up as a person and as a couple than how you respond to each life event together.

Having children is one of those wonderful and celebrated life events that will redefine you as a person, and will redefine your relationship as a couple. As we've seen, many couples unintentionally allow the transition from couple to parent to affect their marital relationship negatively. During the challenging years of parenting, they fail to grow together and to nurture the intimacy and love that brought them together in the first place. The tragic result is a gradual but fatal neglect of their marriage which leads to disillusionment, conflict, unhappiness, and often divorce. It is my hope that you and your spouse will meet the fork in the road that marks the transition from couple to parent with excitement, enthusiasm, and a commitment to keep your marital relationship strong and healthy now and throughout the parenting years. I believe that becoming parents together can draw you closer than ever if you know what to expect and if you invest the necessary time and energy and use the right tools to build a strong marital home—both for you and your spouse as well as for your children. A great marriage to one another is one of the most valuable gifts you can give to your children. Good luck!

Acknowledgments

First, I want to say thank you to my wife, Dana. You are the inspiration for writing this book. I find it difficult to express how much your love, acceptance, support, and encouragement have meant and continue to mean to me. I can imagine no better partner in life than you. I love doing life with you—I just love it. And I love you.

Cal and Ben—you are the greatest! Only when you have children of your own will you understand how much I love you and enjoy being your father. I am so proud of you both. I pray that when the time is right, you will find a wife who is as wonderful as your mom, and I hope that you both work together to stay as in love with one another as your mom and I are with each other.

Mom and Dad—this book is dedicated to you as a fiftieth wedding anniversary gift. Thanks for making it work for a lifetime! I love you both.

To my extended family, friends, and colleagues—you know who you are—thanks for making me laugh, for challenging me, and for your friendship. It means a great deal to me.

A special thanks to my business partner and friend Michael Lyles for making work such a great place and for helping me start my career in Atlanta—you are a true friend. Also a special thanks to my friend Tom Van Gilder for keeping our friendship strong over the years and across the miles. Few people can make me laugh so hard—thanks for that!

I would like to say thank you to my mentor in graduate school, Paul Handal, for investing time in teaching a young and naïve boy from Tennessee. I still remember that you told me the most important thing I would learn in graduate school is to keep learning after I leave, and I try to follow your advice every day.

It has been a real pleasure to work with the professionals at Revell on this book. I want to specifically thank Vicki Crumpton and Paul Brinkerhoff—two true professionals. I've learned a lot from you while working on this project.

Finally, any acknowledgement section would be terribly incomplete and insincere if I did not acknowledge and honor God. I long ago gave up the laughable notion that I could ever do anything to deserve what you've done for me. For every second with my family, for every sunset at the beach, for every great meal, for every word I write, for every breath, and most of all, for grace, I simply drop my head and offer a simple and inadequate but heartfelt . . . *Thank you.* You are amazing.

References

Amato, P. R. & Rivera, F. (1999). Paternal involvement and children's behavior problems. *Journal of Marriage and the Family, 61,* 375–384.

Ball, F. L. J. (1984) *Understanding and satisfaction in marital problem solving: A hermeneutic inquiry.* Unpublished doctoral dissertation, University of California, Berkeley.

Barnes, G. M. (1984). Adolescent alcohol abuse and other problem behaviors: Their relationships and common parental influences. *Journal of Youth and Adolescence, 13,* 329–348.

Belsky, J. & Kelly, J. (1994). *The transition to parenthood.* New York: Delacorte Press.

Belsky, J., Lang, M. E., & Rovine, M. (1985). Stability and change in marriage across the transition to parenthood: The role of violated expectations. *Journal of Marriage and the Family, 47,* 1037–1044.

Belsky, J., Spanier, G., & Rovine, M. (1983). Stability and change in marriage across the transition to parenthood. *Journal of Marriage and the Family, 45,* 567–577.

Carlson, R. (1997). *Don't sweat the small stuff—and it's all small stuff: simple ways to keep the little things from taking over your life.* New York: Hyperion.

Carlson, R. (1998). *Don't sweat the small stuff with your family: simple ways to keep daily responsibilities and household chaos from taking over your life.* New York: Hyperion.

Cloud, H. and Townsend, J. (1992). *Boundaries: when to say yes, when to say no to take control of your life.* Grand Rapids, MI: Zondervan.

Cooksey, E. C. & Fondell, M. M. (1996). Spending time with his kids: Effects of family structure on fathers' and children's lives. *Journal of Marriage and the Family, 58,* 693–707.

Cowan, C. P. (1997). Becoming parents: What has to change for couples? In C. Clulow (Ed.), *Partners becoming parents* (pp. 119–139). Northvale, NJ: Jason Aronson.

Cowan, C. P. & Cowan, P. A. (2000). *When partners become parents: The big life change for couples.* Mahwah, NJ: Lawrence Erlbaum Associates.

Cox, M. J., Paley, B., Payne, C. C., & Burchinal, M. (1999). The transition to parenthood: Marital conflict and withdrawal and parent-infant interactions. In M. J. Cox & J. Brooks-Gunn (Eds.), *Conflict and cohesion in families: Causes and consequences* (pp. 87–104). *The advance in family research series.* Mahwah, NJ: Lawrence Erlbaum Associates.

Deal R. (2002). *The smart stepfamily.* Minneapolis, MN: Bethany.

Feeney, J. A., Hohaus, L., Noller, P., & Alexander, R. P. (2001). *Becoming parents: exploring the bonds between mothers, fathers, and their infants.* Cambridge, UK: Cambridge University Press.

Feldhahn, S. (2004). *For women only: What you need to know about the inner lives of men.* Sisters, OR: Multnomah.

Fields, J. & Casper, L. M. (2001). *America's families and living arrangements: March 2000.* Current population reports, P20–537. U.S. Census Bureau, Washington, DC.

Glick, P. C., & Lin, S.-L. (1986). Recent changes in divorce and remarriage. *Journal of Marriage and the Family, 48,* 737–747.

Gottman, J. M. & Silver, N. (2000). *The seven principles for making marriage work: A practical guide from the country's foremost relationship expert.* New York: Three Rivers Press.

Harley, W. F., Jr. (2001). *His needs, her needs: Building an affair-proof marriage.* Grand Rapids, MI: Revell.

Koestner, R., Franz, C., & Weinberger, J. (1990). The family origins of empathic concern: A twenty-six-year longitudinal study. *Journal of Personality and Social Psychology, 58,* 709–717.

Kurdek, L. A. (1993). Nature and prediction of change in marital quality for first-time parent and nonparent husbands and wives. *Journal of Family Psychology, 6,* 255–265.

Lyles, M. R. (2002). Psychiatric aspects of postpartum mood disorders. *Christian Counseling Today, 10*(4), (19–20).

MacDermid, S. M., Huston, T. L., & McHale, S. M. (1990). Changes in marriage associated with the transition to parenthood: Individual differences as a function of sex-role attitudes and changes in division of labor. *Journal of Marriage and the Family, 52,* 475–486.

Palmer, T. (2003). Perceived husband support as a couple resource in the transition to parenthood. Unpublished doctoral dissertation, The University of North Carolina, Chapel Hill.

Wile, D. B. (1988). *After the honeymoon: How conflict can improve your relationship.* New York: John Wiley & Sons.

Zillman, D. (1994). Cognition-excitation interdependencies in the escalation of anger and angry aggression. In M. Potegal and J. F. Knutson (Eds.), *The dynamics of aggression: Biological and social processes in dyads and groups* (pp. 45–71). Hillsdale, NJ: Erlbaum.

Mark Crawford is a clinical psychologist, team psychologist for the Atlanta Hawks NBA team, consulting psychologist to the Westminster Schools and to Pace Academy, and cofounder of Lyles and Crawford Clinical Consulting, PC. He is the author of *The Obsessive-Compulsive Trap* and a contributor to *The Complete Parenting Book* and *Caring for People God's Way*. Mark and his wife, Dana, have two sons.